GLUTEN-FREE BAKING FOR BEGINNERS

THE ESSENTIAL GUIDE TO SWEET AND SAVORY BAKING

Johnna Wright Perry

PHOTOGRAPHY BY LAURA FLIPPEN

ROCKRIDGE
PRESS

For general information on our other products and services or to obtain technical support, please contact our Customer Care Department within the United States at (866) 744-2665, or outside the United States at (510) 253-0500.

Rockridge Press publishes its books in a variety of electronic and print formats. Some content that appears in print may not be available in electronic books, and vice versa.

TRADEMARKS: Rockridge Press and the Rockridge Press logo are trademarks or registered trademarks of Callisto Media Inc. and/or its affiliates, in the United States and other countries, and may not be used without written permission. All other trademarks are the property of their respective owners. Rockridge Press is not associated with any product or vendor mentioned in this book.

Interior and Cover Designer: Richard Tapp
Art Producer: Sue Bischofberger
Editor: Reina Glenn
Production Editor: Mia Moran
Production Manager: Michael Kay
Photography © 2021 Laura Flippen. Food styling by Laura Flippen

ISBN: Print 978-1-64876-918-4
eBook 978-1-64876-261-1

R0

For all those who said goodbye to gluten and were told you would never break bread across the table again, I'll meet you at the table.

CONTENTS

THE GLUTEN-FREE BAKER

I was diagnosed with celiac disease more than a decade ago, and I still craved recipes for basic treats, like chocolate chip and peanut butter cookies or scones I could share over tea with a new neighbor. When my birthday rolled around, I wanted to be able to make cupcakes, or even a fancy layer cake, to share with friends and family. But most of all, I wanted to be able to make the foods I was used to eating before eliminating gluten—like waffles and pancakes, dinner rolls, muffins to munch on the way out the door. I missed the familiar foods and I struggled to find one cookbook that covered all the essential recipes I wanted.

In searching for gluten-free recipes for these beloved foods, I was fortunate to make the online acquaintance of many skilled gluten-free bakers. With their expertise, they had carved a path for the millions of home cooks who can't have gluten and offered much-needed support and encouragement.

After learning to cook and bake gluten-free, I sought to become one of those bloggers who had been such a lifesaver for me. Not long after starting my own gluten-free food blog, I found myself in culinary centers and grocery stores teaching others all I had learned—both from culinary education programs and trial and error in my own kitchen. Many people I met, new to eating gluten-free, had not been home bakers but suddenly felt pressured to bake from scratch because there were limited gluten-free options in stores (and those available were unappetizing or expensive). Too often, my baking class attendees would be teary-eyed, sharing that they had been unable to bake a birthday cake, or even muffins, for a weekday breakfast because they simply didn't have the gluten-free baking knowledge to do so.

Many eliminate gluten because of a celiac disease diagnosis, nonceliac gluten sensitivity, gluten ataxia, or an autoimmune disease. For some, it is related to an allergy to wheat. Still others find that eating gluten-free eliminates inflammation in their body, or they simply feel better not eating gluten. Whatever your reason for eliminating gluten, learning to bake without it can be intimidating. If you're reading this book, you likely feel similar to my baking class students—at a loss for how to make the baked goods you know and love.

This book is meant to be just like one of my classes, complete with all the information and advice you need to become a successful gluten-free baker. My goal is to teach you how to bake great gluten-free treats—treats so deliciously similar to traditional ones that no one would guess they're gluten-free. I've also tucked into this book all the support and encouragement I can squeeze in between the printed lines. I'm cheering for you to be a successful gluten-free baker, and I'm here to show you how.

CHAPTER ONE

GLUTEN-FREE BAKING 101

Welcome to the world of gluten-free baking. This chapter will give you an understanding of what gluten is, its role in baking, and how you can successfully bake without it plus provide pointers on ingredients and kitchen tools that make gluten-free baking fun and enjoyable. My goal is to help you feel confident in the kitchen so you can bake delicious sweets and savory baked goods everyone will devour.

WHAT IS GLUTEN?

Before we start baking, let's dig into gluten: What is its function in baking? Where is it found in baking ingredients?

Simply put, gluten is the "glue" of baking. Gluten is the common term used for storage proteins, or prolamins, that are insoluble in water and naturally found in wheat, rye, barley, and triticale. The most frequently referenced prolamins are glutenin and gliadin, which are found in wheat and triticale. In addition to glutenin and gliadin, secalins in rye and hordeins in barley are also part of the family of storage proteins referred to as gluten.

Wheat has been cultivated for more than ten thousand years, but it wasn't until the twelfth century that it was milled into the flour that is now used for baking. Barley, much like wheat, has been grown for many centuries. In the world of gluten-containing grains, rye is a relative newcomer, having been grown for just about two thousand years. As much as modern agriculture has changed the way wheat, rye, and barley are planted, harvested, milled, and prepared, what hasn't changed is that each of these grains contains gluten.

GLUTEN'S ROLE IN BAKING

Many characteristics of decadent baked goods can be attributed to gluten. The protein found in gluten-containing grains proves helpful in the following ways:

- When dough is rising, gluten creates a matrix-like net, trapping gas bubbles produced by yeast or another leavening agent, which allows the dough to rise. Look closely at bread and you'll see the network of bubbles in the dough. That's where gluten did its job. In baked goods that do not rise before baking, gas bubbles rise when the batter or dough is baked and are trapped in the protein net created by the gluten.
- Gluten absorbs and retains moisture. This prevents a dry and crumbly result.
- If you've enjoyed the chewiness of sourdough bread or a deep-dish pizza crust, gluten deserves the thanks. It provides elasticity to dough, which translates to chewiness once the baked good comes out of the oven.
- Gluten prevents cookie dough from spreading too much while baking, so a soft, round, chewy cookie comes fresh from the oven.
- Because gluten is a protein, it hardens when baking and creates a firm texture. Similar to how gluten prevents cookies from spreading, it allows breads to develop a firm crust while being light and airy on the inside.

THE CHALLENGE OF BAKING WITHOUT GLUTEN

Baking without gluten can be tricky at first, as you learn to bake without the benefit of gluten's binding capability. It will get easier the more familiar you become with gluten-free ingredients and how they behave in dough and batter. Here are a few common concerns about baking without gluten:

Flavor: This is the number one concern, with just cause. Gluten-free baking often calls for flour made from ingredients like beans and rice, some of which have strong flavors that can leave baked goods with off-putting tastes.

Texture: If your ingredient ratios aren't correct, your gluten-free baked goods can turn out dry, crumbly, or overly dense.

Cost: Whether homemade or store-bought, certified gluten-free baked goods often cost much more than traditional ones because they are milled on dedicated equipment, often in a dedicated facility, which increases overall cost.

Availability: It can be challenging to source and stock the necessary ingredients to make your own gluten-free baked goods. Depending on where you live, your local supermarket may not carry them.

This book addresses each of these issues. It is possible to make gluten-free baked items confidently in your kitchen using readily available ingredients that don't break the bank. I'll teach you how to blend flour mixes with ingredients available at many local supermarkets and show you how to use xanthan and guar gums and leavening agents to help with texture and moisture retention.

It can be confusing to sort out which grains are safe to eat on a gluten-free diet. Following is a list of grains that contain gluten and that **should be avoided**:

- Barley
- Oats*
- Rye
- Spelt
- Triticale
- Wheat, including durum, einkorn, emmer, farina, farro, graham, kamut, semolina, and wheat berries
- Yeast**

*Oats are a naturally gluten-free grain but many times are grown, harvested, transported, or milled with other gluten-containing grains, meaning they may have come into contact with gluten and are no longer suitable for those on a gluten-free diet. Look for oats that are certified gluten-free and grown under a Purity Protocol. This means the oats were grown in dedicated fields, harvested, and milled with dedicated gluten-free equipment, and have not come into contact with other gluten-containing grains.

**Though not a grain, I include yeast because certain types may contain gluten, such as Red Star Platinum yeast. Check the packaging before using and call the manufacturer if you're unsure.

HOW TO MIMIC GLUTEN USING GLUTEN-FREE INGREDIENTS

Gluten has fantastic qualities for baking, giving structure to baked goods, as well as acting as a binder, providing elasticity, and helping retain moisture. Without gluten, the results can be crumbly, dry, and dense. But don't fret, there are many ways to mimic gluten in gluten-free baking.

Most often this is accomplished with a blend of gluten-free flours, such as those made from nuts, rice, or beans. When perusing the gluten-free section of the supermarket, the selection of flours can be overwhelming. Although it may be tempting to purchase only one flour and use it as a direct substitute for wheat flour, this single-flour method rarely works.

Gluten-free baking requires a blend of flours to duplicate most closely the characteristics of gluten in terms of flavor and texture, as well as to produce sufficient protein and starch to provide support, structure, and elasticity. This isn't easy to achieve with any single gluten-free flour.

In addition, you'll add binders, such as guar gum, xanthan gum, and psyllium husk powder, to assist with the elasticity and structure of your baked goods (more on this later).

Because there is not one flour blend or binder perfect for all gluten-free baked goods, I offer three flour blends you can make and use throughout this book.

You will also notice some unique quirks to gluten-free recipes, such as the recipe calling for oil where you might have expected butter. This helps with moisture retention, which can also be a challenge when baking without gluten. Oil does a better job retaining moisture than butter, as butter has a significant amount of water that evaporates during baking.

YOUR GLUTEN-FREE PANTRY

Flours, starches, binders, and ready-made flour blends have a place in the gluten-free pantry, but you don't need every alternative flour on the planet to bake gluten-free. Let's look at what works best, what helps keep your grocery budget manageable, and what's most beginner friendly.

READY-MADE GLUTEN-FREE FLOUR BLENDS

The supermarket shelves today offer many options for ready-made gluten-free flour blends. Although it may seem like the logical first step to reach for one, these blends are not all the same. Some contain binders, whereas others do not. Many are labeled "all-purpose," but won't work well in yeasted breads. And others are high in starches, which may not work for all dietary considerations. However, they can be a great resource if you're just starting your gluten-free baking journey.

I prefer to mix my own gluten-free flour blends for several reasons. First, I have better control of the ingredients used, which directly affects the results of my baked goods. Second is price. The number one reason those on a medically necessary gluten-free diet say they cannot stick with the diet is cost. Mixing your own gluten-free flour blend can be much more affordable than buying a ready-made blend. Mixing your own flour blend helps you to understand more about the available flour options, what each flour does, and how to use it in combination with other flours. I've done the work for you and included my favorite gluten-free flour blends in this chapter (see pages 12–14).

> ### GLUTEN-FREE AND HEALTHY
>
> Gluten-free flour blends are often criticized for being higher in carbs and starches than wheat flour. It is important to remember that baked goods are still baked goods—chocolate chip cookies are meant to be a treat, whether they contain gluten or not. That said, I recognize that you may be looking for healthier options alongside your gluten sensitivity, and for that reason, I've created a Gluten-Free Whole-Grain Flour Blend (page 14) that stars in several recipes, such as Cinnamon Streusel Coffee Cake (page 37), Zucchini Bread (page 66), and Seeded Whole-Grain Rolls (page 129).
>
> You can also use the Gluten-Free Whole-Grain Flour Blend in place of Johnna's Favorite Gluten-Free All-Purpose Flour Blend (page 12) anywhere it appears in this book to make your baked goods a little more nutritious. Plus, several recipes make use of coconut sugar, a less refined, lower gly-cemic index sugar that doesn't compromise the flavor of the end product.

GLUTEN-FREE FLOURS

After a decade of eating gluten-free, I find the following flours to be most useful in my kitchen. These are what I keep on hand to use in blends and, occasionally, on their own.

Almond Flour or Almond Meal: Made by grinding blanched peeled almonds, almond flour is a good replacement for all-purpose wheat flour in many recipes. Almond meal has a coarser grind and sometimes is made with raw almonds that still have their skins on, so the color will be darker. Almond flour and almond meal are denser than most flours, which results in a flatter end product when used alone. Instead, use in combination with other flours, or add more eggs to a recipe that calls for it alone.

Brown Rice Flour: This is a whole-grain flour made from stoneground brown rice that has a bit of a coarse texture. When buying brown rice flour, look for a very fine grind. The flavor of this flour is slightly nutty. It does absorb water more than wheat flour, which leads to dense results, making it best used in a blend.

Cassava Flour: Cassava is also known as yuca and is a root. The entire root is ground into flour that has a very powdery texture. Of all the gluten-free flours, cassava is the easiest to use as a 1:1 weight replacement for all-purpose wheat flour. The flavor is very mild and the color is quite light, so expect your baked goods to be light in color. Cassava is often confused with tapioca starch or flour. Cassava is the entire root, whereas tapioca is only the starch.

Corn Flour or Cornmeal: Both are made from ground corn; however, corn flour is so fine it feels silky between your fingers, and cornmeal is coarse. Both are best used in combination with other gluten-free flours. On the rare occasions they are used alone, binders are especially important.

Millet Flour: This is another whole-grain gluten-free flour. It has a lovely light-brown color, which is helpful in a flour blend to achieve a color like traditional baked goods. In baking, it is very delicate and produces a crumb too fragile to hold up on its own, making it best used with other flours.

Sorghum Flour: This ancient grain makes a whole-grain flour that is slightly nutty and sweet. Although it is possible to use this flour on its own, it is quite absorbent and requires a binder to hold it together.

Sweet White Rice Flour: This flour is made from a high starch, short-grain variety of rice. You may see this called "glutinous rice flour," but don't confuse "glutinous" with the glutens avoided in gluten-free foods. This type of flour works best in flour blends, unless you are making specific noodle or dessert dishes that call for this flour alone.

White Rice Flour: This flour is responsible for the pale color of many gluten-free baked goods. It has a very mild flavor and is quite thirsty, absorbing liquid in recipes. Occasionally you can use white rice flour by itself. I use it in blends as well as on its own for tempura batter.

OTHER GLUTEN-FREE FLOURS TO EXPLORE

The number of available gluten-free flours is on the rise, with new flours being introduced often. Banana flour, coffee cherry flour, and even cricket flour are now available. It isn't necessary to buy all the flours out there, but it is fun to explore. Here are some wild cards to consider:

Amaranth Flour: Made by grinding the seeds of the amaranth plant into flour, this flour is high in fiber, low in carbohydrates, and packed with minerals including magnesium. It is best used in combination with other flours to avoid a dense texture.

Buckwheat Flour: This ingredient is confusing to many because of the word "wheat" in its name. Rest assured, buckwheat flour is a gluten-free flour. It is made from a seed, making it technically grain-free and classified as a pseudocereal. High in fiber and rich with flavor, it is tricky when used alone, quickly becoming thick and sludgy. It is best used in a blend.

Chia Flour: Made by grinding chia seeds into a powder, this flour is not used by itself, as it absorbs up to 10 times its weight in liquid. Used in a flour blend, it acts as a great binder while adding fiber, protein, and omega-3 fatty acids.

Chickpea Flour: This ingredient can be used as a stand-alone flour in recipes such as socca, which makes a nice pizza crust in a short amount of time. In a blend, up to 50 percent can be chickpea flour—the high protein and fiber content are useful in baking.

Coconut Flour: This flour has very little coconut flavor and is very rarely used alone in a recipe. It is among the most absorbent of flours, so do not use this as a 1:1 replacement for all-purpose wheat flour in a recipe.

Hemp Flour: Very high in protein, hemp flour has a deep, nutty flavor. If you enjoy dark artisan breads, this is a fun flour to explore in a flour blend.

Oat Flour: This flour does a great job of mimicking the texture of wheat flour. It is best used in a blend and adds a mild, nutty flavor. You can make your own oat flour by grinding Purity Protocol gluten-free oats in a clean coffee grinder, high-speed blender, or food processor.

Quinoa Flour: This is another pseudocereal, rich in protein and wonderful in baked goods. It is best to use in partnership with other flours to avoid the dense result that comes from a high-protein flour.

Teff Flour: This flour is the key ingredient in injera, a fermented Ethiopian flatbread. There are very few recipes that use teff alone, and it is best used in a blend. It is rich in fiber and calcium and low on the glycemic index scale.

STARCH

Starch plays an important role in mimicking the effects of gluten, adding moisture and texture to help bind ingredients together. In fact, wheat flour is 75 percent starch. The challenge of baking with starches is including enough to provide structure to your baked goods without producing a gritty texture or throwing off the balance of moisture. Here are the starches you'll use most often in gluten-free baking:

Arrowroot: Like cassava flour (see page 7), arrowroot is made from the tuberous root of a plant. It has no flavor, making it my preference for thickening sauces and gravies. It is best to make a slurry with arrowroot and water before adding it to a dish, as it can gel and become gloppy. In baking, it helps create a crunch or crust.

Potato Starch: Not to be confused with potato flour, this starch produces a very tender crumb in baked goods while also providing structure. I use this in Johnna's Favorite Gluten-Free All-Purpose Flour Blend (page 12) for these reasons, plus the flavor is very mild and does not taste like potato.

Tapioca Flour/Starch: This starch adds elasticity and structure to baked goods. It also works well as a thickener for sauces and pie fillings. Occasionally, you will see it used on its own.

BINDERS

Binders are used in gluten-free baked goods to account for the absence of the gluten protein, which creates the elasticity needed for both lightness and structure. Here are the most common binders used in gluten-free baking:

Flaxseed and Chia Seed: These have great binding capability and work in some recipes as an egg substitute. More about these ingredients later.

Guar Gum: Made from guar beans, guar gum is an off-white powder that creates structure and elasticity. It is often used as a substitute for xanthan gum in recipes where the flavor of xanthan is noticeable, or for those who react to xanthan gum.

Psyllium Husk: Psyllium husk, or psyllium powder, is a great source of fiber and absorbs a lot of moisture, which makes it a great choice for gluten-free baked goods, especially breads. In yeasted breads, psyllium husk powder is a superstar, allowing for a much greater rise.

Xanthan Gum: This is the most commonly used binder in gluten-free baking. It is a simple sugar that is fermented from a specific bacteria, most often grown on corn or soy. It lends elasticity and viscosity to gluten-free baked goods.

WEIGHTY MATTERS: MEASURING BY WEIGHT VERSUS VOLUME

Weighing ingredients allows for more accuracy than using measuring cups. Because we all measure differently using measuring cups—scooping ingredients with the measuring cup versus spooning them into the cup, for example, and how full those cups are—produces inconsistencies that can be glaringly inaccurate in gluten-free baking. If you are converting a traditional recipe to gluten-free, it's best to replace flours by their relative weights, not volume. Gluten-free ingredients often vary in weight from their traditional counterparts and cannot be directly interchanged. For example, 1 cup of traditional all-purpose wheat flour weighs 120 grams, whereas the gluten-free flours used in this book range from 96 to 152 grams per cup.

For that reason, I recommend investing in a digital kitchen scale that weighs in grams and ounces (you can find them for less than $20 in big box stores or online). Most digital kitchen scales have a "tare" feature that allows you to zero out the weight of the item you're measuring in, such as the bowl, so you can measure multiple ingredients in the same bowl without including the bowl's weight in the calculation. Simply place an empty bowl on the scale and hit "tare" to reset the measurement to zero. Repeat after each new ingredient you weigh.

On the following pages, you'll find my gluten-free flour blends. When mixing my own flour blends, I look for certified gluten-free ingredients and check the company's statement on batch testing ingredients. I use Anthony's and Authentic Foods brands most often.

JOHNNA'S FAVORITE GLUTEN-FREE ALL-PURPOSE FLOUR BLEND

BLENDS

PREP TIME: 5 minutes
**MAKES 9 CUPS
(152 GRAMS PER CUP)**

**DAIRY-FREE, EGG-FREE,
NUT-FREE, VEGAN**

This is my go-to flour blend—the one I always have on hand to use for my recipes. This is my favorite blend for pancakes, waffles, piecrusts, biscuits, and cookies. I also use this blend for making a roux or a light breading for fried foods.

3 cups (405 grams) brown rice flour

3 cups (504 grams) white rice flour

2 cups (342 grams) potato starch

1 cup (120 grams) tapioca starch

Measure or weigh each individual flour by spooning, not scooping, into the measuring cup and leveling off the top with the back of a knife. Combine in a large bowl and whisk to incorporate. Store in an airtight container. Review the expiration dates on each ingredient's package, and keep your blend no longer than the earliest date.

GLUTEN-FREE BREAD FLOUR BLEND

PREP TIME: 5 minutes

MAKES 12 CUPS

(135 GRAMS PER CUP)

DAIRY-FREE, EGG-FREE, NUT-FREE, VEGAN

This flour blend has more protein than Johnna's Favorite Gluten-Free All-Purpose Flour Blend (page 12) and contains more starch to adjust for the structure needed in baking bread. It performs best in yeasted breads, pizza crusts, and crackers.

4 cups (640 grams) millet flour

4 cups (480 grams) tapioca starch

3 cups (360 grams) sweet white rice flour

1 cup (135 grams) brown rice flour

Measure or weigh each individual flour by spooning, not scooping, into the measuring cup and leveling off the top with the back of a knife. Combine in a large bowl and whisk to incorporate. Store in an airtight container. Review the expiration dates on each ingredient's package, and keep your blend no longer than the earliest date.

GLUTEN-FREE WHOLE-GRAIN FLOUR BLEND

PREP TIME: 5 minutes

**MAKES 9 CUPS
(140 GRAMS PER CUP)**

**DAIRY-FREE, EGG-FREE,
NUT-FREE, VEGAN, WHOLE
GRAIN**

This flour blend contains more fiber than other blends, adding a bit more nutrition to your baking. It works well in artisan breads, galette crusts, and quick breads. You can use this blend in any of this book's recipes that call for Johnna's Favorite Gluten-Free All-Purpose Flour Blend (page 12); however, the inverse is not always true. When a recipe calls for the Gluten-Free Whole-Grain Flour Blend, you might not achieve the same results if you substitute the all-purpose blend.

3 cups (420 grams) sorghum flour

2 cups (320 grams) millet flour

2 cups (270 grams) brown rice flour

2 cups (240 grams) cassava flour

Measure or weigh each individual flour by spooning, not scooping, into the measuring cup and leveling off the top with the back of a knife. Combine in a large bowl and whisk to incorporate. Store in an airtight container. Review the expiration dates on each ingredient's package, and keep your blend no longer than the earliest date.

BLENDS

When adjusting to a new way of eating, switching to sweeteners that are also new to you can result in a major flavor difference in your baked goods. For this reason, I prefer using the sweeteners common to traditional baking, especially in classic recipes. The recipes in this book call for granulated sugar, light brown sugar, and coconut sugar. Coconut sugar is a less refined sugar that has a light, caramel flavor. You can use it as a 1:1 substitution for granulated sugar in many recipes; however, it will give your baked goods a darker, more caramel color.

If you would like to experiment with replacing sugar with honey, maple syrup, agave syrup, or coconut nectar, I suggest starting by replacing only half the sugar to maintain the integrity of the recipes. Especially when using honey, keep a close eye on the oven, as these sugar alternatives can bake faster and cause burning.

BASIC BAKING EQUIPMENT

Gluten-free baking does not require an extensive number of baking supplies, nor any specialty equipment specific to this style of baking. In fact, if you have baked before, you likely own everything you need. Here are the supplies you will find handy in your gluten-free kitchen:

FOR PREPPING

- **Handheld Electric Mixer:** These tools can range in price from very inexpensive to more than $100, but you don't need anything fancy here. I have used the same $25 mixer for years. Choose one that comes with standard beaters and a whisk attachment.
- **Pastry Cutter:** This is my preferred tool for mixing piecrust and cracker doughs.
- **Round Biscuit (3-inch) and Cracker (1½-inch round or fluted) Cutters:** Much easier than cutting out dough circles with a knife.

- **Rubber Spatula:** I have multiple sizes of this tool—from tiny (to scrape out the leftover bits from a small jar) to large (handy for scraping down the sides of a large mixing bowl). Bonus points if these are heatproof silicone.
- **Set of Nested Mixing Bowls:** I prefer stainless steel or tempered glass, like Pyrex. Both are versatile and can be used in places where a heat-tolerant bowl is handy.
- **Set of Small Pinch Bowls:** Handy for measuring and holding a small quantity of dry ingredients before starting a recipe.
- **Wooden Rolling Pin:** Useful for rolling out crusts and crushing ingredients like graham-style crackers before mixing into a recipe. Replace yours if you have used it with gluten-containing ingredients in the past.
- **Wooden Spoons:** If you are gluten-free by medical necessity, replace your wooden spoons if they have been used previously with gluten-containing ingredients.

FOR BAKING

- 8-inch Pullman loaf pan, for baking sandwich bread
- 9-inch pie pan
- 9-inch round cake pans, multiples, for layer cakes
- 9-inch round tart pan
- 9-inch springform pan, for making cheesecake
- 9-inch square metal baking dish
- 9-by-5-inch metal loaf pan
- 12-cup muffin pan
- Large baking sheets, preferably 18 by 13 inches (two will be handy for baking a complete batch of cookies at the same time)
- Nonstick cooking spray
- Parchment paper
- Silicone baking mats sized to match your baking sheets
- Wire cooling racks

10 MOST COMMON FAILS IN GLUTEN-FREE BAKING AND HOW TO FIX OR AVOID THEM

Gluten-free baking is not without its challenges, but there are simple solutions to nearly all the issues you will encounter. Reading through these fails in advance will give you baseline knowledge to prevent or fix these issues when they pop up.

1. MY PIECRUST IS TOO CRUMBLY.

Your piecrust needs more water. Mix in more water, 1 or 2 teaspoons at a time, until the dough pulls together.

2. MY CUPCAKES SANK IN THE MIDDLE WHEN I TOOK THEM OUT OF THE OVEN.

This happens when there is too much air in a batter that is trying hard to bind without gluten. Fix this by preheating the oven 25 degrees warmer than the baking temperature in the recipe, then reduce to the correct temperature when you put the cupcakes in the oven. The initial surge of heat will help the batter bind.

3. MY SANDWICH BREAD DIDN'T STAY DOMED ON TOP ONCE IT COOLED.

This is called overproofing, which happens when dough rises for too long. Follow the rise time in the recipe closely, or try reducing the rise time by 25 percent.

4. MY BREAD DOUGH IS MORE LIKE A BATTER.

This is common with gluten-free bread and isn't cause for panic. Instead of shaping a batter-like dough by hand, consider pouring it into a shaped pan or use a muffin tin to make rolls.

5. I MODIFIED GRANDMA'S CAKE RECIPE TO BE GLUTEN-FREE AND IT TURNED OUT GUMMY.

It could be lacking in binder. Add an extra egg and ½ teaspoon of a binder, like xanthan or guar gum, per each cup of flour used.

6. MY CAKE TURNED OUT VERY DRY.

Gluten-free flours can be very thirsty and absorb a lot of moisture in baked goods. While adding more liquid would make sense, choose the liquid carefully. Butter has a high water content, which evaporates during baking, so instead try oil, yogurt, sour cream, or applesauce.

7. MY COOKIES TURNED OUT GRITTY.

Gluten-free flours can be gritty depending on the grind of the ingredients. Buy flours that are finely ground and avoid grinding flours from whole ingredients at home unless you have a very powerful blender. If you are already using finely ground flours, allow the cookie dough to rest for 10 to 15 minutes before baking to better absorb the liquid in the dough.

8. MY ROLLS TURNED OUT VERY DENSE.

Not enough binder. Add psyllium husk powder to the recipe, 1 teaspoon per cup of flour. It adds fiber that will improve the texture and create a sturdy network within the dough for holding in steam during baking.

9. MY YEASTED BREAD DOUGH DIDN'T RISE.

There could be several causes of this, starting with the yeast. Test your yeast to confirm it's active before you bake by mixing it with 95°F water and 1 teaspoon of sugar. After 10 minutes, you should see the yeast frothing. If not, your yeast is dead and you will need to replace it. Next, make sure the spot where you set your bread to rise is room temperature or warmer and there are no drafts. Bread doesn't rise well in cold temperatures. Finally, if your dough didn't rise well in the oven, trying baking it in a smaller pan, increasing the cooking time, and reducing the oven temperature by 25°F. Gluten-free breads often don't have the same rise as traditional breads and may need to bake for longer because the batter is denser.

10. MY COOKIES SPREAD INTO A PUDDLE.

Your cookies are lacking in binder. Add xanthan or guar gum to the recipe, starting with ½ teaspoon per each cup of flour used. Xanthan and guar gums act as thickeners and stabilizers in baked goods, which is helpful in reinforcing flours that do not contain gluten.

If and when you encounter these issues, remember: You are learning a new way of baking. There will be bumps along the way, but with practice, you will learn how doughs and batters should feel. The more you bake, the easier it gets and, before long, it will be intuitive.

ADAPTING GLUTEN-FREE RECIPES FOR OTHER SENSITIVITIES

Many of us who struggle with gluten also have other dietary intolerances, sensitivities, or allergies to address. For instance, over half those with celiac disease cannot tolerate dairy. It's often an easy substitution or adaptation to make recipes work for those concerns, even if the recipe is also gluten-free. In each chapter of this book, you'll find several recipes that are already dairy-free, egg-free, nut-free, or vegan, and are labeled for easy identification. Gluten-free baking can be for everyone to enjoy!

MAKING A RECIPE DAIRY-FREE

Most gluten-free recipes are easily made dairy-free with simple ingredient substitutions. In baked goods, the flavor difference is not very noticeable and you'll get similar results using these adaptations:

Butter: Use a dairy-free butter substitute, such as Earth Balance sticks, or coconut oil. I prefer refined coconut oil, as it has less of a coconut flavor than unrefined versions.

Cheese: Dairy-free cream cheese and shredded cheeses work well in my recipes.

Whole Milk: Substitute an unsweetened dairy-free milk. I most often use unsweetened almond milk or hemp milk, but you may prefer soy milk or coconut milk.

Yogurt and Sour Cream: Dairy-free yogurts are good substitutes for both these ingredients.

Also, double-check that your nonstick cooking spray is oil only and does not contain dairy.

MAKING A RECIPE EGG-FREE

Both traditional and gluten-free recipes rely on eggs for their binding qualities. Thankfully, we have lots of knowledge in the gluten-free world about using binders other than eggs, which makes removing eggs from recipes much easier. Although egg-centric recipes, such as quiche, will not work well with egg replacements, these substitutions perform just like eggs where they act as a binder:

Applesauce: ¼ cup applesauce replaces 1 egg in many recipes.

Aquafaba: The liquid from a can of chickpeas; 3 tablespoons aquafaba equals 1 egg.

Banana: ¼ cup mashed ripe banana replaces 1 egg.

Chia Egg: Mix 1 tablespoon ground chia seeds in 3 tablespoons hot water to create a slurry that replaces 1 egg. Let sit for 10 minutes to thicken before using.

Flaxseed: Mix 1 tablespoon flaxseed powder in 3 tablespoons hot water to create a slurry that replaces 1 egg. Let sit for 10 minutes to thicken before using.

Psyllium Husk Powder Egg: Mix 1 teaspoon psyllium husk powder in 3 tablespoons hot water to create a slurry that replaces 1 egg. Let sit for 10 minutes to thicken before using.

There are also several commercial egg replacement products available, such as Ener-G Egg Replacer. Carefully check the ingredients of any egg replacement to be certain they are gluten-free.

ABOUT THE RECIPES

The recipes in this book were created with the beginning baker in mind, meaning they are easy to prepare even if you are new to all baking, not just gluten-free baking. Look for the **What You Need to Know** tip at the end of most recipes for some of my best pointers on successful gluten-free baking—a multitude of helpful cues and an occasional word of caution.

Each recipe also has the following labels to help you quickly locate those that work best for your style of eating:

- Dairy-Free
- Egg-Free
- Nut-Free
- Vegan
- Whole Grain

Gluten-free baking is enjoyable and produces tasty treats, especially when you have these helpful nudges along the way. Now, let's get baking!

ESSENTIAL QUICHE
5 WAYS **PAGE 30**

BREAKFAST TREATS

CRANBERRY ORANGE SCONES

PREP TIME: 15 minutes
BAKE TIME: 25 minutes,
plus 10 minutes to cool

MAKES 8 SCONES
DAIRY-FREE OPTION,
EGG-FREE, VEGAN OPTION

Scones are my go-to baked treat to share with a friend over a cup of hot tea. This recipe is the sweeter British version, compared to the savory scone found in Scotland, or the Dutch version that more closely resembles a drop biscuit.

3 cups (456 grams)
    Johnna's Favorite
    Gluten-Free All-Purpose
    Flour Blend (page 12)
⅓ cup (73 grams)
    granulated sugar
2½ teaspoons
    baking powder
1½ teaspoons xanthan gum
1 teaspoon fine sea salt
1½ teaspoons grated
    orange zest (from about
    1 orange)
12 tablespoons (1½ sticks;
    168 grams) cold unsalted
    butter, cut into
    ½-inch cubes
¾ cup (120 grams) dried
    cranberries
1 cup (240 ml) cold
    buttermilk

1. Preheat the oven to 400°F. Line a baking sheet with parchment paper or a silicone baking mat.

2. In a large mixing bowl, stir together the flour blend, sugar, baking powder, xanthan gum, and salt. Stir in the orange zest.

3. Add the butter. Using a fork or pastry cutter, work the butter into the flour until the mixture is crumbly and the butter pieces are pea-size.

4. Add the dried cranberries, gently stirring to keep the crumbly texture.

5. Add the buttermilk a little at a time, stirring just to combine between each addition, until you have a clumpy dough.

6. Turn the dough out onto a sheet of parchment paper or plastic wrap. Lightly knead the dough into one cohesive piece, then press it into a disk that measures 1 inch thick and 9 inches wide. Cut the disk into eight wedges and transfer them to the prepared baking sheet, 2 inches apart.

7. Bake for 23 to 25 minutes, or until the tops are lightly browned. Cool on the baking sheet for 10 minutes before serving.

WHAT YOU NEED TO KNOW: If you don't have buttermilk, make your own! Place 1 tablespoon of apple cider vinegar into a measuring cup, then fill it to the 1-cup mark with milk of your choice. Let stand for 10 minutes before stirring and using in the recipe.

MAKE IT DAIRY-FREE AND VEGAN: Substitute an equal amount of dairy-free butter (such as Earth Balance). You can use almond, soy, or hemp milk for dairy-free buttermilk following the instructions in the preceding tip.

LAZY MORNING PANCAKES

PREP TIME: 15 minutes
COOK TIME: 15 minutes

MAKES 8 PANCAKES
DAIRY-FREE, VEGAN OPTION

These pancakes are my favorite on slow, sleepy mornings. If it's raining, your hair is a mess, and you're still in your pajamas, make these pancakes. However, they are simple and quick enough to make for a weekday breakfast, too.

1½ cups (228 grams)
   Johnna's Favorite
   Gluten-Free All-Purpose
   Flour Blend (page 12)

½ cup (56 grams)
   almond flour

1 tablespoon
   coconut sugar

1 tablespoon
   baking powder

⅛ teaspoon fine sea salt

2 large eggs

1 cup (240 ml) unsweetened
   almond milk

1. In a medium mixing bowl, stir together the flour blend, almond flour, sugar, baking powder, and salt. Set aside.

2. In a small mixing bowl, whisk the eggs, milk, oil, and vanilla bean paste until blended. Add the liquid to the dry ingredients and whisk until there are no lumps in the batter.

3. Heat a large griddle over medium heat. If using a pan prone to sticking, add a bit of cooking spray to the griddle. Scoop the batter onto the griddle, ¼ cup per pancake.

2 tablespoons (30 grams)
coconut oil, melted

1 teaspoon vanilla bean
paste or vanilla extract

Nonstick cooking spray
(optional)

Maple syrup, honey, or
agave, for topping

4. Cook for 2 to 3 minutes, or until bubbles appear around the edges of the pancakes. Flip and cook for another 2 to 3 minutes, until lightly browned on both sides.

5. Serve immediately, topped as desired.

WHAT YOU NEED TO KNOW: These pancakes will be lightly brown when done—a nice tan as opposed to a deep brown. The gluten-free flour blend in this recipe does not brown the way gluten flours brown when making pancakes.

MAKE IT VEGAN: Substitute flax eggs for the eggs in this recipe. In a small bowl, stir together 2 tablespoons (42 grams) flax meal and 6 tablespoons (30 ml) hot water. Let stand for 15 minutes to thicken.

LIGHT AND CRISPY WAFFLES

PREP TIME: 15 minutes
COOK TIME: 30 minutes

MAKES 4 TO 6 WAFFLES
DAIRY-FREE OPTION,
NUT-FREE

A trek around Belgium on a hunt for waffles introduced me to both the traditional Belgian waffle and Liège waffles. I found I liked the sweetness of Liège waffles, which have a bit of crispiness on the outside, but I also liked the light and fluffy texture of the Belgian waffle. This recipe is the perfect marriage of the two—just a touch of sweet, crispy on the outside, and fluffy on the inside.

2 cups (304 grams)
   Johnna's Favorite
   Gluten-Free All-Purpose
   Flour Blend (page 12)
2 tablespoons (28 grams)
   baking powder
2 tablespoons (27.5 grams)
   granulated sugar or
   coconut sugar (24 grams)
2 teaspoons xanthan gum
   or guar gum
½ teaspoon fine sea salt
8 large eggs
1 cup (240 ml) whole milk
½ cup (120 ml) vegetable
   oil or grapeseed oil
1 tablespoon vanilla bean
   paste or vanilla extract
Nonstick cooking spray
Maple syrup, agave, or
   honey, for topping

1. In a large mixing bowl, stir together the flour blend, baking powder, sugar, xanthan gum, and salt to combine.

2. Separate the eggs, placing the yolks on top of the flour mixture and the whites in a small mixing bowl. Add the milk, oil, and vanilla bean paste to the flour mixture and stir to combine the ingredients.

3. Preheat the waffle iron and spray it with cooking spray.

4. Using a handheld electric mixer on medium speed, whip the egg whites for 4 to 5 minutes until they form stiff peaks. Gently fold the whites into the flour mixture, taking care not to knock the air out of the egg white mixture.

5. Pour the batter into the hot waffle iron. The amount will vary based on your iron, but many Belgian waffle makers hold ¾ cup of batter per waffle. Close the lid and cook for 5 to 8 minutes, or until golden brown.

6. Using a fork or tongs, transfer the waffle to a plate. Repeat with the remaining batter.

7. Serve the waffles immediately with desired toppings.

WHAT YOU NEED TO KNOW: An easy way to test waffles for doneness without opening the waffle iron is to watch the steam coming from the waffle maker. It will begin to slow when the waffle is done.

MAKE IT DAIRY-FREE: This recipe works well with almond, soy, and hemp milks. Substitute the dairy-free milk of your choice for the whole milk in equal amounts.

ESSENTIAL QUICHE 5 WAYS

PREP TIME: 30 minutes
BAKE TIME: 45 minutes,
plus 5 minutes to cool

MAKES ONE 9-INCH QUICHE

**DAIRY-FREE OPTION,
NUT-FREE**

Quiche is a brunch favorite in my kitchen—a dish I can make ahead and reheat or serve at room temperature. I like the ease of this recipe, which includes a simple formula for switching up the filling ingredients and requires no blind baking of the crust. If you like a creamier quiche, use 1 cup (230 ml) milk and ½ cup (120 ml) heavy cream.

1 single Piecrust (page 92)

4 large eggs

1½ cups (360 ml) whole
   milk or unsweetened
   almond milk

½ teaspoon fine sea salt

1½ cups (about 120 grams,
   weight varies by type)
   shredded cheese
   of choice

1 cup (weight varies)
   flavorful mix-ins (optional)

1. Preheat the oven to 375°F.

2. For the piecrust: Following steps 1 to 6 on page 92, roll the piecrust into a 10-inch circle and press it into a 9-inch pie pan. Trim the edges, or finish in a decorative manner if you'd like, then set the pie pan on a baking sheet.

3. In a large mixing bowl, whisk together the eggs, milk, and salt until well blended.

4. Stir in the cheese.

5. Layer 1 cup of mix-ins into the piecrust (if using). Then, gently pour the egg mixture over them.

6. Place the quiche, still on the baking sheet, into the oven. Bake for 40 to 45 minutes, or until the filling is set in the middle. Let cool for 5 minutes before slicing and serving.

MEDITERRANEAN QUICHE: ½ cup (15 grams) packed fresh spinach, ¼ cup (28.75 grams) oil-packed sundried tomatoes, and ¼ cup (25 grams) Kalamata olives, sliced; use 1 cup (80 grams) shredded Cheddar and ½ cup (56 grams) crumbled feta or goat cheese crumbles for the cheese

 SAUSAGE AND MUSHROOM QUICHE: ¾ cup (86.25 grams) cooked sausage crumbles and ¼ cup (32.5 grams) sautéed sliced mushrooms

 DENVER OMELET QUICHE: ½ cup (75 grams) cubed ham, ¼ cup (36.25 grams) sautéed diced green bell pepper, and ¼ cup (21.75 grams) sautéed diced yellow onion

 BROCCOLI QUICHE: 1 cup (71 grams) broccoli florets; use 1½ cups (120 grams) shredded mozzarella for the cheese

 QUICHE LORRAINE: ¾ cup (60 grams) crumbled cooked bacon and ¼ cup (21.75 grams) sautéed diced yellow onion; use 1½ cups (180 grams) shredded Swiss or Gruyère for the cheese

MAKE IT DAIRY-FREE: Substitute an equal amount of unsweetened almond, flax, or hemp milk for the dairy milk, and an equal amount of dairy-free shredded cheese.

DUTCH BABY
OR GERMAN PANCAKE

PREP TIME: 10 minutes
BAKE TIME: 18 minutes

MAKES 4 SERVINGS

**DAIRY-FREE OPTION,
NUT-FREE**

Whether you call this a Dutch baby, a German pancake, or a Bismarck, this popover-style dish makes an impressive breakfast indulgence. Puffy and brown on the edges, it will fall in the middle when removed from the oven, leaving the perfect spot to fill with fruit, powdered sugar, and syrup. You may notice that this recipe contains no xanthan or guar gum. That's because the eggs puff more on their own.

1 tablespoon
  unsalted butter
4 large eggs
¾ cup (180 ml) whole milk
¾ cup (114 grams) Johnna's
  Favorite Gluten-Free
  All-Purpose Flour Blend
  (page 12)
1 teaspoon vanilla bean
  paste or vanilla extract
Fruit of choice, for topping
Powdered sugar, maple
  syrup, agave, or honey,
  for topping

1. Preheat the oven to 425°F.

2. Place the butter in an 8-inch square metal baking dish or an 8-inch round cast-iron pan.

3. Crack the eggs into a blender and blend on medium speed for 15 to 20 seconds until frothy. Add the milk, flour blend, and vanilla bean paste. Blend for 15 to 20 seconds until well combined.

4. Place the baking dish into the oven for 1 to 2 minutes, letting the pan heat and the butter melt. Once the butter melts, remove the pan from the oven and gently roll the melted butter around to coat the bottom and sides of the pan. Carefully pour out any excess butter.

5. Pour the batter into the pan and place it into the oven. Cook for 15 to 18 minutes, rotating the pan halfway through the baking time, until the middle is set.

6. Remove from the oven and cut into wedges or squares. Top with fruit and sweetener of choice. Serve immediately.

WHAT YOU NEED TO KNOW: This recipe works best in a cast-iron pan or metal baking dish. Although it will work in an oven-safe glass baking dish, the Dutch baby will not puff as tall. It will still be delicious, though!

MAKE IT DAIRY-FREE: Use equal amounts of dairy-free butter substitute (such as Earth Balance) and dairy-free milk (such as almond, soy, or hemp milk). I use unsweetened almond milk in this recipe. Use another milk, such as flax or hemp, if nuts are an issue for you.

CREPES WITH BANANA

AND CHOCOLATE-HAZELNUT FILLING

PREP TIME: 15 minutes, plus 30 minutes to chill
COOK TIME: 10 minutes

MAKES 10 CREPES

DAIRY-FREE OPTION,
NUT-FREE OPTION

When I had to eliminate gluten from my diet, the foods I missed the most were those I had enjoyed while traveling. Watching a giant crepe made on a large, flat griddle at a street side crêperie in Paris is a favorite memory. The cook pours out just the right amount of batter and then spreads it into a perfectly thin crepe using a wooden tool reminiscent of a rake. Fret not, no special equipment is required to whip up this recipe at home and enjoy a virtual vacation from the comfort of your own kitchen.

1 large egg

½ cup (76 grams) Johnna's Favorite Gluten-Free All-Purpose Flour Blend (page 12)

⅓ cup plus 1 tablespoon (95 ml) whole milk

¼ cup (60 ml) water

1 tablespoon plus 1 teaspoon (19 grams) unsalted butter, melted

1 tablespoon granulated sugar

½ teaspoon vanilla bean paste or vanilla extract

1. In a blender, combine the egg, flour blend, milk, water, melted butter, granulated sugar, and vanilla bean paste. Pulse for 10 to 15 seconds until well combined. Pour the batter into a sealable container and refrigerate for 30 minutes. This allows the air bubbles that formed while blending to dissipate and thickens the batter to the perfect consistency for crepes.

2. Heat a 5- or 6-inch skillet over medium heat. If the skillet is not nonstick, lightly coat it with cooking spray before making each crepe.

CONTINUED

Nonstick cooking spray
  (optional)
⅓ cup (99 grams)
  chocolate-hazelnut
  spread
3½ bananas, sliced, divided
2 tablespoons (15 grams)
  powdered sugar

3. Pour 2 tablespoons (1 ounce; 28 grams) of the crepe batter into the center of the skillet and very quickly tilt the pan in a circular motion to spread the batter evenly around the skillet. Cook for 30 seconds. Using a thin metal spatula, gently flip the crepe and cook for about 15 seconds on the other side, or until very lightly browned. Transfer the crepe to a plate. Repeat with the remaining batter.

4. Spread each crepe with 1½ teaspoons of the chocolate-hazelnut spread and top with one-third of a sliced banana. Fold or roll the crepe, then sprinkle with powdered sugar and serve.

WHAT YOU NEED TO KNOW: This batter can be made up to 24 hours in advance and refrigerated until ready to use.

MAKE IT DAIRY-FREE: Substitute equal amounts of dairy-free butter (such as Earth Balance) and unsweetened almond milk, if nuts are not an issue. There are also dairy-free chocolate-hazelnut spreads available, including Nocciolata and Artisana Organics brands.

MAKE IT NUT-FREE: For a completely nut-free version, substitute chocolate-sunflower seed butter for the chocolate-hazelnut spread, like 88 Acres brand, or Soom brand chocolate sweet tahini spread.

CINNAMON STREUSEL

COFFEE CAKE

PREP TIME: 15 minutes
BAKE TIME: 37 minutes

**MAKES 1 (8-INCH)
SQUARE CAKE
DAIRY-FREE OPTION,
WHOLE GRAIN**

The sweet aroma of this coffee cake while it bakes is guaranteed to wake up anyone sleeping in and draw them into the kitchen with the promise of warm streusel.

FOR THE STREUSEL

½ cup (70 grams)
   Gluten-Free Whole-Grain
   Flour Blend (page 14)
⅓ cup (64 grams)
   coconut sugar
2 tablespoons (28 grams)
   unsalted butter, at room
   temperature
1 teaspoon ground
   cinnamon

FOR THE CAKE

Butter or nonstick
   cooking spray
1½ cups (210 grams)
   Gluten-Free Whole-Grain
   Flour Blend (page 14)
½ cup (96 grams)
   coconut sugar
2 teaspoons baking powder
Dash fine sea salt

TO MAKE THE STREUSEL

1. In a small bowl, using a fork, stir together the flour blend, sugar, butter, and cinnamon until crumbly. Set aside.

TO MAKE THE CAKE

2. Preheat the oven to 350°F. Lightly grease an 8-inch square baking dish with butter.

3. In a large mixing bowl, stir together the flour blend, sugar, baking powder, and salt to combine. Make a well in the center of the dry ingredients and add the eggs, milk, and vanilla bean paste. Stir well to combine.

4. Pour half the cake batter into the prepared baking dish. Sprinkle with all but 2 tablespoons of the streusel. Pour the remaining batter over the streusel, then sprinkle the top with the reserved 2 tablespoons of streusel.

CONTINUED

2 large eggs

¾ cup (180 ml) whole milk

1 teaspoon vanilla bean
   paste or vanilla extract

FOR THE GLAZE

½ cup (60 grams)
   powdered sugar

1 tablespoon whole milk

½ teaspoon vanilla bean
   paste or vanilla extract

5. Bake for 35 to 37 minutes, or until a toothpick inserted into the center of the cake comes out clean. Set on a wire rack to cool while making the glaze.

TO MAKE THE GLAZE

6. Sift the powdered sugar into a small bowl. Stir in the milk and vanilla bean paste until smooth. Drizzle over the top of the warm cake.

7. Slice the coffee cake into nine pieces and serve while warm, or at room temperature.

WHAT YOU NEED TO KNOW: This recipe uses coconut sugar, which is made from the flower of the coconut tree. In addition to being lower on the glycemic index, coconut sugar has a light caramel flavor that works well in recipes with warming spices and deep, rich flavors. You can use granulated sugar in this recipe, but it won't have that crucial caramel flavor.

MAKE IT DAIRY-FREE: Substitute equal amounts of dairy-free butter (such as Earth Balance) and unsweetened almond milk, if nuts are not an issue.

FLAKY BISCUITS

PREP TIME: 20 minutes
BAKE TIME: 18 minutes, plus 5 minutes to cool

MAKES 7 BISCUITS

NUT-FREE

Serve these biscuits hot from the oven with butter and jam or beneath a creamy blanket of sausage gravy. This recipe makes big, flaky biscuits with visible layers in the dough— perfect for slicing in half to make a ham and egg breakfast sandwich.

3¾ cups (570 grams) Johnna's Favorite Gluten-Free All-Purpose Flour Blend (page 12)

4 teaspoons (18 grams) baking powder

1 tablespoon granulated sugar

1½ teaspoons xanthan gum

1½ teaspoons fine sea salt

12 tablespoons (1½ sticks; 168 grams) cold unsalted butter, cut into ¼-inch cubes

3 large eggs

1 cup (240 ml) plus 3 tablespoons (45 ml) buttermilk, divided

1. Preheat the oven to 375°F. Line a baking sheet with parchment paper or a silicone baking mat.

2. In a large mixing bowl, stir together the flour blend, baking powder, sugar, xanthan gum, and salt.

3. Using a pastry blender or fork, cut the butter into the dry ingredients until the pieces are pea-size. Make a well in the center of this mixture.

4. In a medium bowl, whisk together the eggs and 1 cup (240 ml) of buttermilk. Pour the wet ingredients into the well in the flour mixture and stir to form a soft, wet dough.

CONTINUED

5. Cover a clean work surface with a large piece of plastic wrap. Turn the dough out onto the plastic wrap and cover with an equal size piece of plastic wrap. Press the dough into a 12-inch square. Remove the top piece of plastic wrap and fold the left side of the dough toward the middle. Then, fold the right side of the dough to the middle, forming a book. Fold this in half (close the book), bringing the left and right sides together to form a rectangle. Cover with plastic wrap and pat the dough down into a 1-inch-thick slab.

6. Using a 3-inch round biscuit cutter, press it straight down into the dough and pull straight up to form the biscuits. Do not twist the cutter, as this inhibits the flaky layers. Gather the remaining dough scraps into one last biscuit, pressing with the cutter briefly to form the correct shape. Place the biscuits on the prepared baking sheet and brush the tops with the remaining 3 tablespoons (45 ml) of buttermilk.

7. Bake for 16 to 18 minutes, or until the tops turn light brown. Cool the biscuits on the baking sheet for 5 minutes before serving.

WHAT YOU NEED TO KNOW: Using cold butter is the key to flaky biscuits. Those pea-size pieces in the dough help create a light, airy crumb.

HELPFUL HINT: If your biscuit cutter sticks to the dough, dip it in some flour blend between each biscuit. Additionally, if your dough starts to get soft because the butter is warmed from working it, refrigerate for 10 minutes or so until the butter firms up again.

CLASSIC BLUEBERRY MUFFINS

PREP TIME: 15 minutes
BAKE TIME: 27 minutes, plus at least 5 minutes to cool

MAKES 12 MUFFINS

DAIRY-FREE OPTION, NUT-FREE

Among the challenges of gluten-free baking is getting moisture content just right, so the baked goods aren't too moist and dense or so dry that they crumble into tiny pieces when you pick them up. These muffins are perfectly moist yet also light and fluffy. Enjoy these warm from the oven!

Nonstick cooking spray (optional)

3 cups (456 grams) Johnna's Favorite Gluten-Free All-Purpose Flour Blend (page 12)

1½ cups (165 grams) granulated sugar

4 teaspoons baking powder

2 teaspoons xanthan gum or guar gum

½ teaspoon fine sea salt

⅔ cup (80 ml) whole milk

⅔ cup (80 ml) vegetable oil

2 large eggs

3 teaspoons vanilla bean paste or vanilla extract

2 cups fresh or frozen blueberries

1. Preheat the oven to 400°F. Line a 12-cup muffin tin with paper liners, or coat it with the cooking spray.

2. In a large mixing bowl, whisk together the flour blend, sugar, baking powder, xanthan gum, and salt to combine.

3. In a small mixing bowl, whisk together the milk, oil, eggs, and vanilla bean paste to blend. Add the wet ingredients to the dry ingredients, stirring just to combine.

4. Rinse the blueberries, whether fresh or frozen, and gently blot dry with a paper towel. Carefully fold the blueberries into the batter. Fill each prepared muffin cup with a scant ⅓ cup of batter.

CONTINUED

5. Bake for 25 to 27 minutes, or until the tops are lightly browned and a toothpick inserted into the center of a muffin comes out clean. Cool the muffins in the muffin tin for 5 minutes before serving, or transfer to a wire rack to cool completely.

WHAT YOU NEED TO KNOW: Washing and gently blotting the blueberries dry before folding them into the batter helps keep the batter from turning purple. Folding carefully (as opposed to stirring) is essential for the same reason.

MAKE IT DAIRY-FREE: Replace the whole milk with an equal amount of nondairy milk. Unsweetened almond milk, if nuts are not an issue, works well in this recipe. Hemp and soy milks are also good substitutes, but they make the muffins a bit less fluffy.

CUT-OUT SUGAR
COOKIES **PAGE 54**

CHAPTER THREE

COOKIES AND BARS

CLASSIC CHOCOLATE CHIP COOKIES

PREP TIME: 15 minutes
BAKE TIME: 12 minutes, plus
5 minutes to cool
MAKES 24 COOKIES
**DAIRY-FREE OPTION,
NUT-FREE**

This classic chocolate chip cookie recipe will fool even the pickiest eater—no one will know it's not the chocolate chip cookie of days past. Crunchy on the edges, chewy in the center, it's perfectly sweet with chocolate and the lingering richness of brown sugar. When I need a quick batch of cookies to take to a gathering or to lift up a friend, this is my go-to recipe.

1½ cups (228 grams) Johnna's Favorite Gluten-Free All-Purpose Flour Blend (page 12)

1 teaspoon baking soda

½ teaspoon xanthan gum

¼ teaspoon fine sea salt

8 tablespoons (1 stick; 112 grams) unsalted butter, at room temperature

½ cup (120 grams) packed light brown sugar

¼ cup (55 grams) granulated sugar

1 large egg

1 teaspoon vanilla bean paste or vanilla extract

1 cup (170 grams) semisweet chocolate chips

1. Preheat the oven to 350°F. Line two baking sheets with parchment paper or silicone baking mats.

2. In a large mixing bowl, whisk together the flour blend, baking soda, xanthan gum, and salt to combine. Set aside.

3. In a medium mixing bowl, using a handheld electric mixer on medium speed, cream together the butter, brown sugar, and granulated sugar until smooth. Add the egg and vanilla bean paste and mix until just combined. Add the butter mixture to the flour mixture and stir together with a wooden spoon until combined.

4. Stir in the chocolate chips.

5. Scoop the dough onto the prepared baking sheets, measuring 1 heaping tablespoon per cookie, about 12 cookies to a sheet spaced about 2½ inches apart.

6. Bake for 10 to 12 minutes, or until the edges are lightly browned but the middle is still soft. Cool for 5 minutes on the baking sheet before serving.

7. Transfer the extra cookies to a wire rack to cool completely before storing in an airtight container.

WHAT YOU NEED TO KNOW: If you're having trouble getting your cookies to turn out right, your baking soda might be stale. In this recipe, fresh baking soda prevents the cookies from spreading too far. If yours has been open for more than 6 months, test the freshness of your baking soda (and baking powder, while you're at it) by dropping a little into hot water. If it does not fizz, it's time to toss it. (And when you get a new container, write the date on it after opening.)

MAKE IT DAIRY-FREE: Substitute equal amounts of dairy-free butter (such as Earth Balance) and dairy-free chocolate chips (such as Enjoy Life brand).

OATMEAL COOKIES

PREP TIME: 20 minutes
BAKE TIME: 11 minutes, plus
5 minutes to cool

MAKES 36 COOKIES
WHOLE-GRAIN OPTION

When oatmeal cookies were first created, they were promoted as a health food. While I won't go so far as to call a cookie a health food, these cookies are packed with fiber thanks to the Purity Protocol gluten-free oats. I've also lightened the sugar content by using coconut sugar. These cookies are soft and chewy in the center with a crunchy edge—just like you remember—only without the gluten.

1¼ cups (2½ sticks; 280 grams) unsalted butter, at room temperature

¾ cup (180 grams) packed light brown sugar

½ cup (96 grams) coconut sugar

1 large egg

1 teaspoon vanilla bean paste or vanilla extract

1½ cups (228 grams) Johnna's Favorite Gluten-Free All-Purpose Flour Blend (page 12)

1 teaspoon xanthan gum or guar gum

1 teaspoon baking soda

1 teaspoon ground cinnamon

1. Preheat the oven to 375°F. Line two baking sheets with parchment paper or silicone baking mats.

2. In a large mixing bowl, using a handheld electric mixer on medium speed, cream together the butter, light brown sugar, and coconut sugar until smooth. Add the egg and vanilla bean paste and mix until well combined.

3. Add the flour blend, xanthan gum, baking soda, cinnamon, nutmeg, and salt. Using a large wooden spoon, combine the ingredients.

4. Stir in the oats and raisins (if using). Scoop the dough onto the prepared baking sheets, measuring 1 heaping tablespoon per cookie, about 12 cookies to a sheet, spaced about 2½ inches apart. You will have one baking sheet's worth of dough left over.

¼ teaspoon
  ground nutmeg
¼ teaspoon fine sea salt
3 cups (252 grams) Purity
  Protocol gluten-free oats
1 cup (160 grams) raisins
  (optional)

5. Bake for about 9 minutes, for a soft, chewy cookie with lightly brown edges, or about 11 minutes, for a crispy cookie with darker edges. Cool for 5 minutes on the baking sheet before serving. Wait until one of the baking sheets has cooled to room temperature to bake the last batch of cookies. (You may be tempted to reuse your warm baking sheet right after your first batch of cookies to bake the final batch, but this is not ideal. It's best to use a room-temperature baking sheet to get a consistent result. Using a warm baking sheet could make the cookies spread too much.)

6. Transfer the extra cookies to a wire rack to cool completely before storing in an air-tight container.

WHAT YOU NEED TO KNOW: If you live in a house divided over whether to include raisins in your oatmeal cookies, there is an easy solution. Split the cookie dough into two equal batches after adding the oats and only add raisins to half of the dough.

MAKE IT WHOLE GRAIN: This recipes works equally well with my Gluten-Free Whole-Grain Flour Blend (page 14).

PEANUT BUTTER COOKIES

PREP TIME: 15 minutes
BAKE TIME: 8 minutes, plus
5 minutes to cool

MAKES 24 COOKIES

DAIRY-FREE, EGG-FREE, VEGAN

If you're like me, avoiding gluten might not be the only food restriction you, or your family or friends, have to contend with. I wanted a cookie recipe I could share with all my friends, regardless of their diets, but creating peanut butter cookies that were both satisfying to all and gluten-free, dairy-free, and egg-free was a challenge. I tried several options to replace the egg and finally landed on an ingredient that didn't alter the flavor or the texture of the cookie—pumpkin! This cookie has the sweet crunch of a traditional peanut butter cookie with just a touch of chewiness.

1¼ cups (275 grams) granulated sugar, divided

⅔ cup (101 grams) Johnna's Favorite Gluten-Free All-Purpose Flour Blend (page 12)

2 teaspoons baking soda

½ teaspoon fine sea salt

1½ cups (390 grams) smooth peanut butter

⅓ cup (81 grams) pure pumpkin puree

1½ teaspoons vanilla bean paste or vanilla extract

1. Preheat the oven to 350°F. Line two baking sheets with parchment paper or silicone baking mats.

2. In a large mixing bowl, stir together 1 cup (220 grams) of sugar, the flour blend, baking soda, and salt. Add the peanut butter, pumpkin, and vanilla bean paste. Mix to combine, creating a stiff dough.

3. Place the remaining ¼ cup (55 grams) of sugar in a small bowl.

4. Roll the dough into 1-inch balls and coat them in the sugar. Place the cookies on the prepared baking sheets, 12 cookies to a sheet, spaced about 2 inches apart.

5. Press the back of a fork into each cookie ball, then rotate the fork 90 degrees and make a second indent, creating a crisscross pattern on the top of each cookie.

6. Bake for about 8 minutes, or until the center of each cookie is no longer glossy. Cool for 5 minutes on the baking sheet before serving.

7. Transfer the extra cookies to a wire rack to cool completely before storing in an airtight container.

WHAT YOU NEED TO KNOW: Common vegan egg substitutes include flax or chia eggs, bananas, or applesauce, but pumpkin also works as an egg substitute in baked goods with denser textures, like cookies.

VARIATION TIP: If you prefer a crunchier cookie, bake the cookies on parchment sheets. Baking on silicone baking mats results in a softer, chewier peanut butter cookie.

SNICKERDOODLE COOKIES

PREP TIME: 20 minutes
BAKE TIME: 13 minutes, plus 5 minutes to cool

MAKES 36 COOKIES
DAIRY-FREE OPTION, NUT-FREE

Snickerdoodles are very nostalgic to me. Shared often for classroom birthday parties growing up, I always picture them sitting on top of a napkin, placed on my desktop by a classmate's parent. I love the cinnamon and sugar exterior combined with the slightly cakey interior that is both soft and chewy. You don't need to be celebrating a birthday to enjoy these cookies.

2½ cups (380 grams) Johnna's Favorite Gluten-Free All-Purpose Flour Blend (page 12)

3 teaspoons ground cinnamon, divided

½ teaspoon baking powder

½ teaspoon xanthan gum

8 tablespoons (1 stick; 112 grams) unsalted butter, at room temperature

1 cup (220 grams) plus 1 tablespoon granulated sugar, divided

2 large eggs

2 tablespoons (30 ml) whole milk

1 teaspoon vanilla bean paste or vanilla extract

1. Preheat the oven to 375°F. Line two baking sheets with parchment paper or silicone baking mats.

2. In a large mixing bowl, stir together the flour blend, 1 teaspoon of cinnamon, the baking powder, and xanthan gum. Set aside.

3. In a medium mixing bowl, using a handheld electric mixer on medium speed, cream together the butter, 1 cup (220 grams) of sugar, the eggs, milk, and vanilla bean paste until well combined. Add this mixture to the flour mixture and stir to combine.

4. In a small mixing bowl, stir together the remaining 1 tablespoon of sugar and remaining 2 teaspoons of cinnamon.

5. Roll the dough into 1-inch balls, then coat them in the cinnamon sugar. Place the cookies on the prepared baking sheets, 12 cookies to a sheet, spaced about 2 inches apart. You will have one baking sheet's worth of dough left over.

6. Bake for 11 to 13 minutes, or until lightly browned on the edges. Cool for 5 minutes on the baking sheet before serving. Wait until one of the baking sheets has cooled to room temperature to bake the last batch of cookies.

7. Transfer the extra cookies to a wire rack to cool completely before storing in an airtight container.

WHAT YOU NEED TO KNOW: You may be tempted to reuse your warm baking sheet right after your first batch of cookies to bake the final batch, but this is not ideal. It's best to use a room-temperature baking sheet to get a consistent result. Using a warm baking sheet could make the cookies spread too much.

MAKE IT DAIRY-FREE: Substitute equal amounts of dairy-free butter (such as Earth Balance) and unsweetened dairy-free milk. This recipe works well with almond milk, if nuts are not an issue, and hemp milk.

CUT-OUT SUGAR COOKIES

If you enjoy decorating cut-out cookies for the holidays, you'll love these! While they are lovely unadorned, these cookies make the perfect base for decorating with colored sugar, sprinkles, or royal icing. This was one of the first classic recipes I modified to be gluten-free and soon after won a baking competition with it. Only after receiving my award did I learn the judges had no idea the cookies were gluten-free.

PREP TIME: 1 hour, plus 30 minutes to chill
BAKE TIME: 10 minutes, plus at least 5 minutes to cool

MAKES ABOUT 24 COOKIES (DEPENDING ON SHAPE)

DAIRY-FREE OPTION, NUT-FREE

3 cups (456 grams) Johnna's Favorite Gluten-Free All-Purpose Flour Blend (page 12)

1½ teaspoons guar gum

1½ teaspoons baking powder

½ teaspoon fine sea salt

1 cup (220 grams) granulated sugar

1 cup (2 sticks; 224 grams) unsalted butter, at room temperature

1 large egg

1 teaspoon vanilla bean paste or vanilla extract

1. In a large mixing bowl, whisk together the flour blend, guar gum, baking powder, and salt to combine.

2. In a small mixing bowl, using a handheld electric mixer on medium speed, cream together the sugar and butter until smooth. Add the egg and vanilla bean paste and mix until combined. Add this mixture to the flour mixture and stir to form a smooth dough.

3. Split the dough into two equal parts. Place each on a piece of plastic wrap and flatten into a disk. Wrap with plastic wrap and refrigerate for at least 30 minutes.

4. Preheat the oven to 350°F. Line two baking sheets with parchment paper or silicone baking mats.

5. To roll out the dough, unwrap the plastic from one dough disk and lay the plastic wrap on a flat surface. Place the dough on top of the plastic and cover it with another piece of plastic wrap. Using a rolling pin, roll the dough into a sheet ⅓ inch thick.

6. Using cookie cutters, cut the dough into any shapes you like. Transfer the cut cookies onto the prepared baking sheets, spacing them about 1 inch apart.

7. Bake for 8 to 10 minutes, or until lightly browned on the edges. Cool on the baking sheet for 5 minutes before serving. If decorating, transfer to a wire rack to cool completely before icing.

WHAT YOU NEED TO KNOW: Decorate these cookies with sprinkles or colored sugars right after they come out of the oven—no icing necessary. Press the decoration gently into the warm cookies to ensure it sticks.

MAKE IT DAIRY-FREE: Substitute an equal amount of dairy-free butter (such as Earth Balance).

RASPBERRY SHORTBREAD BARS

These are the prettiest little bars and one of my favorite gifts to take to a friend's dinner party. They are the perfect sweet (but not too sweet) treat for a tired host to enjoy after the guests have left, or the next morning with a hot beverage. The shortbread crust is rich with butter and the raspberry filling has just a hint of tartness to pair with the rich crust. They look like an indulgence from a fancy bakery, but you can make them yourself in no time.

PREP TIME: 10 minutes
BAKE TIME: 33 minutes, plus 20 minutes to cool

MAKES 9 TO 12 BARS
DAIRY-FREE OPTION, NUT-FREE

Nonstick cooking spray
8 tablespoons (1 stick; 112 grams) unsalted butter, at room temperature
¼ cup (55 grams) granulated sugar
1 teaspoon vanilla bean paste or vanilla extract
1½ cups (228 grams) Johnna's Favorite Gluten-Free All-Purpose Flour Blend (page 12)

1. Preheat the oven to 350°F. Coat an 8-inch square baking pan with the cooking spray.

2. In a large mixing bowl, stir together the butter, granulated sugar, and vanilla bean paste until creamy. Add the flour blend and xanthan gum and mix until just crumbly.

3. Firmly press half the mixture into the bottom of the prepared baking pan, forming a crust.

4. Carefully spread the jam over the crust. Crumble the remaining half of the crust mixture over the jam.

CONTINUED

½ teaspoon xanthan gum

½ cup (160 grams) raspberry jam

2 tablespoons (15 grams) powdered sugar (optional)

5. Bake for 31 to 33 minutes, or until the top starts to lightly brown. Cool completely on a wire rack for about 20 minutes before cutting into 9 or 12 squares.

6. Sprinkle with the powdered sugar (if using) before serving.

7. Store leftovers in an airtight container at room temperature.

WHAT YOU NEED TO KNOW: These bars are delicious with other flavors of jam. Try strawberry, apricot, or blackberry.

MAKE IT DAIRY-FREE: Substitute an equal amount of dairy-free butter (such as Earth Balance).

MONSTER BARS

PREP TIME: 15 minutes
BAKE TIME: 20 minutes,
plus 20 minutes to cool

MAKES 9 TO 12 BARS
WHOLE GRAIN

Monster bars are a Midwest classic, most often baked in a large batch on a jelly roll pan. I've adapted this recipe to yield a smaller batch and baked it in a square pan to get a solid bar shape. If you're looking for a sweet treat when traveling, these are both durable and filling.

Nonstick cooking spray

¾ cup (195 grams) smooth peanut butter

2 tablespoons (28 grams) unsalted butter, at room temperature

2 large eggs

½ cup (96 grams) coconut sugar

¼ cup (35 grams) Gluten-Free Whole-Grain Flour Blend (page 14)

1 teaspoon baking soda

½ cup (120 grams) chocolate chips

½ cup (84 grams) chocolate candies (such as M&Ms)

2¼ cups (189 grams) Purity Protocol gluten-free oats

1. Preheat the oven to 325°F. Coat an 8-inch square baking pan with the cooking spray.

2. In a large mixing bowl, stir together the peanut butter, butter, and eggs until smooth.

3. Add the sugar, flour blend, and baking soda, stirring to combine.

4. Stir in the chocolate chips and candies. Add the oats in two batches, stirring to combine with each addition. This creates a crumbly mixture. Press the mixture firmly into the prepared baking pan.

5. Bake for 15 to 20 minutes, or until the center no longer looks soft. Cool completely on a wire rack for 20 minutes before cutting into 9 or 12 squares.

WHAT YOU NEED TO KNOW: Substitute other combinations of ingredients in place of the chocolate chips and chocolate candies. I like white chocolate chips and dried cranberries, or butterscotch and dark chocolate chips.

LEMON SQUARES

PREP TIME: 30 minutes
BAKE TIME: 42 minutes,
plus 30 minutes to cool

MAKES 9 TO 12 SQUARES

NUT-FREE

This recipe incorporates the bright, tart flavor of lemon with the sweet flavor of shortbread. A creamy, thick lemon curd sits atop a delicate shortbread crust that is irresistibly buttery. I always plan to eat just one of these squares when I bake them as a gift for a friend who loves all things lemon, then I end up making a second batch because it's not possible to stop at just one!

FOR THE CRUST

8 tablespoons (1 stick;
   112 grams) unsalted
   butter, at room
   temperature
¼ cup (55 grams)
   granulated sugar
1 cup (152 grams) Johnna's
   Favorite Gluten-Free
   All-Purpose Flour Blend
   (page 12)
Dash fine sea salt

TO MAKE THE CRUST

1. Preheat the oven to 350°F.

2. In a medium mixing bowl, using a handheld electric mixer on medium speed, cream together the butter and granulated sugar until smooth. Add the flour blend and salt, mixing until just combined. Transfer the dough to an 8-inch square baking pan, pressing it into the bottom and ½ inch up the sides, forming a crust.

3. Bake for about 12 minutes, until lightly browned, then cool on a wire rack while you prepare the filling.

3 large eggs, at room
temperature

1 cup (220 grams)
granulated sugar

½ cup (76 grams) Johnna's
Favorite Gluten-Free
All-Purpose Flour Blend
(page 12)

½ cup (120 ml) freshly
squeezed lemon juice

1 teaspoon grated lemon
zest (from 1 small lemon)

2 tablespoons (15 grams)
powdered sugar

TO MAKE THE FILLING

4. In a medium mixing bowl, whisk together
the eggs, granulated sugar, flour blend, lemon
juice, and lemon zest until well combined
and smooth with no clumps. Pour the filling
over the crust.

5. Bake for 25 to 30 minutes, or until the filling is set. Cool completely on a wire rack
for about 30 minutes, then dust with
the powdered sugar and cut into 9 or
12 squares to serve.

WHAT YOU NEED TO KNOW: When baking lemon
squares, you may notice a thin white layer form
over the top of the lemon filling. This is related to
the freshness of the eggs. Eggs that have been in
the refrigerator longer than a few days are more
likely to form this white layer, whereas fresh eggs
are less likely to, as air hasn't permeated the
eggshell yet. Either way, it won't affect the taste
of the bars and won't be noticeable once they are
dusted with powdered sugar.

HELPFUL HINT: Use freshly squeezed lemon juice
for the most intense lemon flavor. Bottled juice
can sometimes have a bitter aftertaste.

FUDGY BROWNIES

PREP TIME: 15 minutes
BAKE TIME: 38 minutes,
plus 30 minutes to cool

MAKES 9 TO 12 BROWNIES
NUT-FREE

Whether you like the corner and edge pieces or the center pieces, you'll love this brownie recipe. I recommend baking in a metal rather than glass pan for brownies, as it heats up faster and cooks more evenly.

Nonstick cooking spray
8 tablespoons (1 stick;
    112 grams) unsalted
    butter, melted
1½ cups (330 grams)
    granulated sugar
¾ cup (60 grams)
    unsweetened
    cocoa powder
1 teaspoon vanilla bean
    paste or vanilla extract
3 large eggs
¾ cup (114 grams) Johnna's
    Favorite Gluten-Free
    All-Purpose Flour Blend
    (page 12)
1 teaspoon baking powder
1 teaspoon instant coffee
    or espresso granules
½ teaspoon fine sea salt
¼ teaspoon xanthan gum

1. Preheat the oven to 350°F. Coat an 8-inch-square baking pan with the cooking spray.

2. In a large mixing bowl, stir together the melted butter, sugar, and cocoa powder until the sugar begins to dissolve. Add the vanilla bean paste and eggs, stirring again to combine.

3. Add the flour blend, baking powder, instant coffee, salt, and xanthan gum and stir to combine. Spoon the batter into the prepared baking pan.

4. Bake for 33 to 38 minutes, or until the brownies start pulling away from the sides of the pan and a toothpick inserted into the center comes out with just a few crumbs attached.

5. Cool completely on a wire rack for about 30 minutes before cutting into 9 or 12 brownies.

BLONDIES

PREP TIME: 20 minutes
BAKE TIME: 25 minutes, plus 30 minutes to cool

MAKES 9 TO 12 BLONDIES

NUT-FREE

Creating a recipe for gluten-free blondies that allowed the middle to bake completely without the edges burning was a challenge. After many batches, I discovered the trick: whip the batter before baking.

Nonstick cooking spray

8 tablespoons (1 stick; 112 grams) unsalted butter, melted

¾ cup (180 grams) packed light brown sugar

1 large egg

2 teaspoons vanilla bean paste or vanilla extract

1½ cups (228 grams) Johnna's Favorite Gluten-Free All-Purpose Flour Blend (page 12)

½ teaspoon baking powder

½ teaspoon fine sea salt

¼ teaspoon baking soda

½ cup (120 grams) white chocolate chips

½ cup (120 grams) milk chocolate chips

1. Preheat the oven to 350°F. Lightly coat an 8-inch square baking pan with the cooking spray.

2. In a large mixing bowl, stir together the melted butter, light brown sugar, egg, and vanilla bean paste.

3. In a small mixing bowl, whisk the flour blend, baking powder, salt, and baking soda. Add the flour mixture to the butter mixture and stir to combine well.

4. Using a handheld electric mixer on high speed, whip the batter for two minutes until light and fluffy. Incorporating air into the batter allows for even baking.

5. Stir in the white and milk chocolate chips. Pour the batter into the prepared pan.

6. Bake for 22 to 25 minutes, or until the edges are golden brown and starting to pull away from the pan and a toothpick inserted into the center comes out clean. Cool completely on a wire rack for about 30 minutes before cutting into 9 or 12 blondies.

VERY VANILLA CUPCAKES
WITH VANILLA BEAN BUTTER-
CREAM FROSTING **PAGE 70**

CHAPTER FOUR

QUICK BREADS, CAKES, AND CUPCAKES

ZUCCHINI BREAD

PREP TIME: 30 minutes
BAKE TIME: 1 hour
20 minutes, plus
1 hour to cool

**MAKES 1
(9-BY-5-INCH) LOAF**
**DAIRY-FREE, NUT-FREE
OPTION, WHOLE GRAIN**

Zucchini bread is my favorite quick bread to make when summer's zucchini crop becomes abundant. When friends and neighbors share their ample supply, I like to make a loaf for my family and a second loaf to thank the neighbor for supplying the main ingredient. Give it a try and see if baskets of zucchini begin to appear on your doorstep every year.

Nonstick cooking spray

3 small zucchini

1½ cups (330 grams) granulated sugar

⅔ cup (160 ml) grapeseed oil or vegetable oil

4 large eggs

1 tablespoon vanilla bean paste or vanilla extract

3 cups (420 grams) Gluten-Free Whole-Grain Flour Blend (page 14)

2 teaspoons baking soda

1 teaspoon xanthan gum

1 teaspoon ground cinnamon

¾ teaspoon fine sea salt

½ teaspoon baking powder

¼ teaspoon ground cloves

½ cup (64 grams) chopped walnuts (optional)

1. Preheat the oven to 350°F. Coat a 9-by-5-inch loaf pan with cooking spray and set aside.

2. Using a box grater or the shredding attachment on a food processor, grate the zucchini using the second largest cutting size. You should have about 3 cups (450 grams). Place in a large mixing bowl.

3. Add the sugar, oil, eggs, and vanilla bean paste to the zucchini. Stir until well mixed.

4. Stir in the flour blend, baking soda, xanthan gum, cinnamon, salt, baking powder, and cloves until well mixed. Fold in the walnuts (if using) and pour the batter into the prepared loaf pan.

5. Bake for 1 hour 10 minutes to 1 hour 20 minutes, or until a toothpick inserted into the center of the loaf comes out clean. Place the loaf pan on a wire rack to cool for 10 minutes. Gently loosen the loaf around the edges of the pan with a knife and tip out the loaf to cool completely, about 1 hour, on the rack before slicing.

WHAT YOU NEED TO KNOW: It is not necessary to peel the zucchini before shredding. If your zucchini are very large, you may wish to halve them vertically, then halve again and use a spoon to scoop out the seeds, as they will be predominant in the loaf.

MAKE IT NUT-FREE: Instead of walnuts, raisins or dried cranberries work well in this recipe.

BANANA BREAD

PREP TIME: 20 minutes
BAKE TIME: 1 hour
10 minutes, plus
45 minutes to cool

**MAKES 1
(9-BY-5-INCH) LOAF
DAIRY-FREE OPTION,
NUT-FREE, WHOLE GRAIN**

*This classic quick bread is baked weekly in
my kitchen. It's the perfect accompaniment
to breakfast or brunch and makes a great
snack. Plus, it's the best use for overripe
bananas.*

Nonstick cooking spray

4 tablespoons (56 grams)
unsalted butter, at room
temperature

¼ cup (60 ml) grapeseed oil
or vegetable oil

1 cup (220 grams)
granulated sugar
or (192 grams)
coconut sugar

2 large eggs

3 ripe bananas, mashed
with a fork

1 teaspoon ground
cinnamon

2 cups (280 grams)
Gluten-Free Whole-Grain
Flour Blend (page 14)

1 teaspoon baking powder

1 teaspoon baking soda

1 teaspoon fine sea salt

1 teaspoon xanthan gum

1. Preheat the oven to 325°F. Coat a 9-by-5-inch
loaf pan with the cooking spray. Set aside.

2. In a large mixing bowl, using a handheld electric mixer on medium speed, cream together
the butter, oil, and sugar until smooth.

3. One at a time, add the eggs, mixing to incorporate after each addition.

4. Add the bananas and cinnamon, mixing
to combine.

5. In a medium mixing bowl, whisk together the
flour blend, baking powder, baking soda, salt,
and xanthan gum. A little at a time, add the
dry ingredients to the wet mixture, incorporating the mixer after each addition. Pour the
batter into the prepared loaf pan.

6. Bake for 1 hour to 1 hour 10 minutes, or until a toothpick inserted into the center of the loaf comes out clean. Place the loaf pan on a wire rack to cool for 15 minutes. Gently loosen the loaf around the edges with a knife and tip out the loaf to cool completely, about 30 minutes, on the wire rack before slicing.

WHAT YOU NEED TO KNOW: Always have bananas ripe and ready for banana bread by freezing bananas when they get ripe. Peel the ripe bananas, place in an airtight container, and freeze. Thaw the bananas to room temperature before using in this recipe.

MAKE IT DAIRY-FREE: Substitute an equal amount of dairy-free butter (such as Earth Balance).

VERY VANILLA CUPCAKES

WITH VANILLA BEAN BUTTERCREAM FROSTING

PREP TIME: 45 minutes
BAKE TIME: 22 minutes,
plus 30 minutes to cool

MAKES 12 CUPCAKES
DAIRY-FREE, NUT-FREE

This cupcake recipe is so versatile—it's the recipe I use most often when I need to take a dozen cupcakes to a friend, donate to a community bake sale, or celebrate at home. Vanilla is easy to dress up with any frosting flavor and fun toppings like sprinkles, candies, or fresh fruit.

FOR THE CUPCAKES

1¾ cups (266 grams)
   Johnna's Favorite
   Gluten-Free All-Purpose
   Flour Blend (page 12)
1½ teaspoons
   baking powder
½ teaspoon baking soda
½ teaspoon fine sea salt
¼ teaspoon xanthan gum
1 cup (220 grams)
   granulated sugar
¾ cup (180 grams)
   dairy-free yogurt
⅓ cup (80 ml) unsweetened
   dairy-free milk
4 tablespoons (56 grams)
   dairy-free butter, at room
   temperature

TO MAKE THE CUPCAKES

1. Preheat the oven to 350°F. Line a 12-cup muffin tin with silicone or paper liners.

2. In a medium mixing bowl, whisk together the flour blend, baking powder, baking soda, salt, and xanthan gum to combine.

3. In a large mixing bowl, using a handheld electric mixer on medium speed, cream together the sugar, yogurt, milk, butter, eggs, oil, and vanilla bean paste until smooth.

4. Gradually mix in the dry mixture until there are no clumps. Scoop a scant ⅓ cup of batter into each cupcake well.

5. Reduce the oven temperature to 325°F.

2 large eggs

¼ cup (60 ml) grapeseed oil
or vegetable oil

1 tablespoon vanilla bean
paste or vanilla extract

FOR THE FROSTING

1 cup (2 sticks; 224 grams)
dairy-free butter, at room
temperature

1 teaspoon vanilla bean
paste or vanilla extract

3 cups (360 grams)
powdered sugar, sifted

1 to 2 tablespoons
(15 to 30 ml) unsweetened
dairy-free milk

6. Bake for 20 to 22 minutes, or until a toothpick inserted into the center of a cupcake comes out clean. Place the tin on a wire rack and let the muffins cool for 15 minutes. Remove the cupcakes and place them directly on the rack for about 15 minutes to cool completely.

TO MAKE THE FROSTING

7. While the cupcakes cool, in a medium mixing bowl, using a handheld electric mixer on low speed, mix the butter and vanilla bean paste.

8. Slowly add the powdered sugar, ½ cup (60 grams) at a time, mixing well after each addition, until well combined. Mix in the milk, 1 tablespoon at a time, until the frosting reaches your preferred consistency.

9. Using an offset spatula or butter knife, frost the completely cooled cupcakes.

WHAT YOU NEED TO KNOW: Heating the oven to 350° F, then reducing the temperature to 325° F helps your cupcakes have a more domed shape.

CHOCOLATE CUPCAKES

WITH PEANUT BUTTER FROSTING

PREP TIME: 45 minutes
BAKE TIME: 22 minutes,
plus 30 minutes to cool

MAKES 12 CUPCAKES

If you are a fan of peanut butter cups, this is the cupcake for you. The chocolate cake is rich and the peanut butter frosting is creamy—the perfect marriage for a dessert.

FOR THE CUPCAKES

1¼ cups (190 grams)
Johnna's Favorite
Gluten-Free All-Purpose
Flour Blend (page 12)

½ cup (40 grams)
unsweetened
cocoa powder

½ teaspoon xanthan gum

1¼ cups (275 grams)
granulated sugar

5 tablespoons (70 grams)
unsalted butter, at room
temperature

⅓ cup (80 ml) grapeseed
oil or vegetable oil

1¼ teaspoons vanilla bean
paste or vanilla extract

1 teaspoon instant coffee
granules

3 large eggs

⅔ cup (160 ml) water

TO MAKE THE CUPCAKES

1. Preheat the oven to 350°F. Line a 12-cup muffin tin with silicone or paper liners.

2. In a medium mixing bowl, whisk together the flour blend, cocoa powder, and xanthan gum. Set aside.

3. In a large mixing bowl, using a handheld electric mixer on medium speed, combine the granulated sugar, butter, oil, vanilla bean paste, and instant coffee. One at a time, add the eggs, mixing to incorporate after each addition.

4. Add one-third of the dry mixture to the wet mixture, then one-third of the water, and blend with the mixer on medium speed. Repeat until all the dry ingredients and water are added. Scoop a scant ⅓ cup of batter into each cupcake well.

5. Reduce the oven temperature to 325°F.

FOR THE FROSTING

1 cup (2 sticks; 224 grams)
unsalted butter, at room
temperature

¾ cup (195 grams) smooth
peanut butter

2 teaspoons vanilla bean
paste or vanilla extract

3 cups (360 grams)
powdered sugar, sifted

2 to 3 tablespoons
(30 to 45 ml) whole milk

6. Bake for 20 to 22 minutes, or until a toothpick inserted into the center of a cupcake comes out clean. Place the pan on a wire rack to cool for 15 minutes. Remove the cupcakes and place them on the rack for about 15 minutes to cool completely.

TO MAKE THE FROSTING

7. While the cupcakes cool, in a medium mixing bowl, using a handheld electric mixer on medium speed, beat the butter until fluffy.

8. Add the peanut butter and mix until well combined.

9. Add the vanilla bean paste, then add the powdered sugar, a little at a time (to keep the sugar from flying around your kitchen), mixing to combine after each addition. One tablespoon at a time, mix in the milk until the frosting reaches your preferred consistency.

10. Using an offset spatula or butter knife, frost the completely cooled cupcakes.

WHAT YOU NEED TO KNOW: These cupcakes look extra fun when topped with half a peanut butter cup. Be cautious when choosing a peanut butter cup though, as not all are gluten-free. The unwrapped mini peanut butter cups and some holiday shapes contain gluten. Always read labels and check with the manufacturer if you are unsure.

SPICE CUPCAKES

WITH MAPLE FROSTING

PREP TIME: 45 minutes
BAKE TIME: 22 minutes,
plus 30 minutes to cool

MAKES 12 CUPCAKES

NUT-FREE, WHOLE GRAIN

These cupcakes are warming and flavorful thanks to a blend of seasonal spices and perfectly sweet maple frosting. One bite and you'll be dreaming of autumn in Vermont. Try these with a cup of hot tea.

FOR THE CUPCAKES

5 tablespoons plus
   1 teaspoon (75 grams)
   unsalted butter, at room
   temperature
¾ cup (180 grams) packed
   light brown sugar
½ cup (110 grams)
   granulated sugar
⅓ cup (80 ml) grapeseed
   oil or vegetable oil
3 large eggs
⅔ cup (160 ml) buttermilk
2 teaspoons vanilla bean
   paste or vanilla extract
1⅔ cups (232 grams)
   Gluten-Free Whole-Grain
   Flour Blend (page 14)
1 teaspoon ground
   cardamom
1 teaspoon ground
   cinnamon

TO MAKE THE CUPCAKES

1. Preheat the oven to 350°F. Line a 12-cup muffin tin with silicone or paper liners.

2. In a large mixing bowl, using a handheld electric mixer on medium speed, cream together the butter, light brown sugar, and granulated sugar until smooth. Add the oil, then the eggs, one at a time, mixing to combine after each addition. Add the buttermilk and vanilla bean paste and mix well.

3. In a medium mixing bowl, whisk together the flour blend, cardamom, cinnamon, xanthan gum, ginger, salt, baking soda, baking powder, and nutmeg to combine. Add the dry ingredients to the wet ingredients and mix to combine. Scoop a scant ⅓ cup of batter into each cupcake well.

4. Reduce the oven temperature to 325°F.

1 teaspoon xanthan gum

½ teaspoon ground ginger

½ teaspoon fine sea salt

½ teaspoon baking soda

½ teaspoon baking powder

¼ teaspoon
  ground nutmeg

1 cup (2 sticks; 224 grams)
  unsalted butter, at room
  temperature

2 tablespoons (40 grams)
  maple syrup

1 teaspoon maple extract

3 cups (360 grams)
  powdered sugar, sifted

1 to 2 tablespoons
  (15 to 30 ml) whole milk

5. Bake for 20 to 22 minutes, or until a tooth-pick inserted into the center of a cupcake comes out clean. Place the tin on a wire rack to cool for 15 minutes. Remove the cupcakes and place them directly on the rack for about 15 minutes to cool completely.

TO MAKE THE FROSTING

6. While the cupcakes cool, in a medium mixing bowl, using a handheld electric mixer on medium speed, beat the butter until fluffy. Add the maple syrup and maple extract, mixing until well combined.

7. A little at a time (to keep the sugar from flying around your kitchen), add the powdered sugar, mixing to combine after each addition. One tablespoon at a time, mix in the milk until the frosting reaches your preferred consistency.

8. Using an offset spatula or butter knife, frost the completely cooled cupcakes.

WHAT YOU NEED TO KNOW: For the best flavor, use pure maple syrup, not a syrup artificially flavored with maple. The same is true with maple extract—look for one labeled pure maple flavor.

CARROT CAKE
WITH CREAM CHEESE FROSTING

PREP TIME: 30 minutes
BAKE TIME: 32 minutes, plus 30 minutes to cool

MAKES 1 (9-INCH) CAKE
DAIRY-FREE OPTION

Carrot cake used to feel daunting to me, but this recipe is perfect for both a weeknight dessert and a special occasion. In many recipes, vanilla bean paste and vanilla extract are interchangeable. For the cream cheese frosting in this recipe, I recommend using vanilla bean paste. Your frosting will not only taste of rich vanilla flavor, it will also have visible flecks of vanilla bean. A simple swap like this can really elevate your baking.

FOR THE CAKE

Nonstick cooking spray
1 cup (220 grams) granulated sugar
⅔ cup (160 ml) grapeseed or vegetable oil
2 large eggs
1 teaspoon vanilla bean paste or vanilla extract
1 cup (152 grams) Johnna's Favorite Gluten-Free All-Purpose Flour Blend (page 12)
1 teaspoon ground cinnamon
1 teaspoon baking soda

TO MAKE THE CAKE

1. Preheat the oven to 350°F. Line two (9-inch) cake pans with parchment paper and lightly coat them with the cooking spray. Set aside.

2. In a large mixing bowl, using a handheld electric mixer on medium speed, combine the granulated sugar, oil, eggs, and vanilla bean paste until well combined but not yet frothy.

CONTINUED

¾ teaspoon fine sea salt

½ teaspoon xanthan gum

2½ cups (230 grams) shredded carrot (from about 4 large carrots)

½ cup (64 grams) walnuts, coarsely chopped

FOR THE FROSTING

8 ounces (240 grams) cream cheese, at room temperature

12 tablespoons (1½ sticks; 168 grams) unsalted butter, at room temperature

½ teaspoon vanilla bean paste or vanilla extract

½ teaspoon fine sea salt

2 cups (240 grams) powdered sugar, sifted

3. In a medium mixing bowl, whisk together the flour blend, cinnamon, baking soda, salt, and xanthan gum to combine. Add this to the wet ingredients and mix on medium speed to combine the batter.

4. Using a wooden spoon, fold in the carrots and walnuts. Divide the batter evenly between the prepared pans.

5. Bake for 32 minutes, or until a toothpick inserted in the center of each cake comes out with only small crumbs attached. Set the pans on wire racks to cool for 15 minutes. Then, use a butter knife to gently loosen the cakes around the edges and tip the cakes out onto the racks to cool completely for about 15 minutes before assembling.

TO MAKE THE FROSTING

6. In a medium bowl, using a handheld electric mixer on medium speed, combine the cream cheese, butter, vanilla bean paste, and salt until smooth.

7. A little at a time (to keep the sugar from flying around your kitchen), add the powdered sugar, mixing into a smooth frosting.

8. Choose a cake stand or plate. Cut four parchment paper strips and arrange them around the edges. These will fit just under the edges of the cake, then be removed for a clean presentation once the cake is frosted.

9. Gently turn the first cake upside-down and place it on the stand so it sits in the center of the parchment strips. Remove the parchment circle from the bottom of the cake. Using an offset spatula or butter knife, spread a thick layer of frosting over the first layer of the cake. Repeat with the second layer, stacking it upside down as well.

10. Frost the entire cake with a layer of frosting, then decorate as you like. (I like to press extra chopped walnuts around the edges of the cake.)

11. Pull the parchment strips away from the cake. Serve immediately or refrigerate until ready to serve.

WHAT YOU NEED TO KNOW: For a simpler, less time-consuming version of this cake, skip the layers. Bake in a 9-inch square baking pan for 40 to 45 minutes, cool it, and frost the cake right in the pan. (You'll only need half the amount of frosting if you choose this method.)

MAKE IT DAIRY-FREE: Substitute equal amounts dairy-free butter (such as Earth Balance) and dairy-free cream cheese (such as Kite Hill or Daiya).

PINEAPPLE UPSIDE-DOWN CAKE

PREP TIME: 45 minutes
BAKE TIME: 40 minutes, plus 1 hour to cool

MAKES 1 (9-INCH) CAKE
DAIRY-FREE OPTION, NUT-FREE

Near my hometown, there was a cafeteria that had been open since the 1930s. In addition to the classic meals and every vegetable you can imagine, the shelves were lined with single servings of the most delightful cakes, pies, and breads. I always ordered the pineapple upside-down cake. Now, I bake it at home and you can, too.

Nonstick cooking spray

3 tablespoons (45 ml) melted unsalted butter

½ cup (96 grams) packed light brown sugar

7 pineapple rings

4 maraschino cherries, halved

1½ cups (228 grams) Johnna's Favorite Gluten-Free All-Purpose Flour Blend (page 12)

2 teaspoons baking powder

½ teaspoon xanthan gum

¼ teaspoon fine sea salt

6 tablespoons (¾ stick; 84 grams) unsalted butter, at room temperature

1. Preheat the oven to 350°F. Lightly coat a 9-inch square baking pan with the cooking spray. Set aside.

2. Pour the melted butter into the pan. Sprinkle the light brown sugar over the butter. Place the pineapple rings side by side in the pan, cutting the last one to fill the space. Place half a cherry, cut-side up, in the center of each pineapple ring. Set aside.

3. In a small mixing bowl, whisk together the flour blend, baking powder, xanthan gum, and salt to combine.

4. In a large mixing bowl, using a handheld electric mixer on medium speed, combine the butter, granulated sugar, egg, vanilla bean paste, and milk.

5. Add the dry ingredients and mix to combine into a batter. Gently pour the batter over the pineapple rings.

⅔ cup (147 grams)
  granulated sugar
1 large egg
¾ teaspoon vanilla bean
  paste or vanilla extract
⅔ cup (160 ml) whole milk

6. Bake for 38 to 40 minutes, or until a toothpick inserted into the center of the cake comes out clean. Set the pan on a wire rack to cool for 15 minutes, then gently loosen the cake by running a knife around the edges.

7. Place a serving plate upside-down on top of the cake pan and quickly turn them both over so the baking pan is now on top of the plate. Let sit for 15 minutes to let the butter and sugar mixture soak into the cake.

8. Remove the baking pan and let the cake cool completely, about 30 minutes, before serving. Cut into 8 squares, each featuring a pineapple ring.

WHAT YOU NEED TO KNOW: It is important to flip the cake out of the pan after it has cooled for only 15 minutes. Any longer and you risk the pineapple rings and cherries sticking to the bottom of the pan.

MAKE IT DAIRY-FREE: Substitute equal amounts of dairy-free butter (such as Earth Balance) and dairy-free milk. Unsweetened almond milk works well in this recipe (if nuts are not a concern).

FLOURLESS CHOCOLATE TORTE

PREP TIME: 30 minutes
BAKE TIME: 40 minutes,
plus at least 1 hour to cool

MAKES 1 (9-INCH) TORTE

**DAIRY-FREE OPTION,
NUT-FREE**

When I first began eating a gluten-free diet, I mostly made recipes that were naturally gluten-free. This flourless chocolate torte is a good example. Some flourless chocolate torte recipes require separating eggs and using a double boiler for melting chocolate. Neither of those are required here, making it simple enough to enjoy for any occasion.

Nonstick cooking spray

5 tablespoons (25 grams) unsweetened cocoa powder, divided, plus more for topping (optional)

1 cup (2 sticks; 224 grams) unsalted butter, cut into ½-inch pieces

¼ cup (60 ml) heavy (whipping) cream

8 ounces (240 grams) bittersweet chocolate, coarsely chopped

5 large eggs

1 cup (220 grams) granulated sugar

Powdered sugar or whipped cream, for topping (optional)

1. Preheat the oven to 350°F. Coat a 9-inch springform pan with the cooking spray and dust it with 1 tablespoon of cocoa powder. Shake out any excess and set aside.

2. In a small saucepan over medium heat, combine the butter and heavy cream. Heat, stirring, until the butter melts. Add the chocolate and stir until melted. Remove from the heat and set aside.

3. In a medium mixing bowl, whisk together the eggs, sugar, and remaining 4 tablespoons (20 grams) of cocoa powder to blend. In a slow stream, whisk in the butter mixture until combined. Pour the batter into the prepared pan.

4. Bake for 35 to 40 minutes, or until there is very little jiggle in the middle. Place the pan on a wire rack to cool for 1 hour, then gently run a knife around the edges to loosen the cake. Release the springform ring. Transfer the cake back to the rack to cool completely before serving.

5. Sprinkle the powdered sugar or cocoa powder (if using) over the top of the cake immediately before serving, or top with a dollop of whipped cream (if using).

WHAT YOU NEED TO KNOW: Use a high-quality chocolate for this recipe. Splurge on bar chocolate that has a large percentage of cacao, like the 85 percent dark chocolate bar from Christopher Elbow Chocolates, or the 88 percent super dark bar from Askinosie Chocolate.

MAKE IT DAIRY-FREE: Substitute an equal amount of dairy-free butter (such as Earth Balance). For the heavy (whipping) cream, use canned coconut cream (such as Thai Kitchen brand), not to be confused with coconut milk.

DOUBLE-CHOCOLATE

BIRTHDAY LAYER CAKE

PREP TIME: 1 hour
BAKE TIME: 22 minutes,
plus 30 minutes to cool

MAKES 1 (9-INCH)
3-TIER CAKE

DAIRY-FREE, EGG-FREE,
NUT-FREE OPTION, VEGAN

When the occasion is as special as your birthday, you deserve a fancy, decadent cake. I created this recipe for my birthday, wanting to bake a vegan cake that reminded me of one I used to get at a boutique bakery my family visited only on special occasions. If you want to make this cake extra fancy, add strawberries between the layers.

FOR THE CAKE

Nonstick cooking spray

2 tablespoons (12 grams)
chia seed powder

6 tablespoons (90 ml)
hot water

1 cup (152 grams) Johnna's
Favorite Gluten-Free
All-Purpose Flour Blend
(page 12)

1 cup (112 grams)
almond meal

2 cups (384 grams)
coconut sugar

⅔ cup (53 grams)
unsweetened
cocoa powder

1 teaspoon baking powder

1 teaspoon baking soda

1 teaspoon sea salt

TO MAKE THE CAKE

1. Preheat the oven to 350°F. Line three (9-inch) cake pans with parchment paper and lightly coat them with the cooking spray. Set aside.

2. In a small bowl, stir together the chia seed powder and hot water. Let sit for 10 minutes to gel.

3. Meanwhile, in a large mixing bowl, stir together the flour blend, almond meal, coconut sugar, cocoa powder, baking powder, baking soda, salt, and guar gum to combine.

4. In a medium mixing bowl, stir together the milk, yogurt, oil, vanilla bean paste, and instant coffee until well combined. Stir in the chia mixture. Add the wet mixture to the dry mixture, stirring well to combine. Pour 2 generous cups of batter into each prepared cake pan. Evenly divide any remaining batter.

1 teaspoon guar gum

1¼ cups (300 ml)
  unsweetened
  dairy-free milk

¾ cup (180 grams)
  dairy-free yogurt, plain
  or vanilla

⅓ cup (80 ml) grapeseed or
  vegetable oil

2 tablespoons (30 grams)
  vanilla bean paste or
  (30 ml) vanilla extract

2 teaspoons instant coffee
  granules

5. Bake the cakes for 18 to 22 minutes, or until a toothpick inserted into the center of each cake comes out clean. Set the pans on wire racks to cool for 15 minutes. Then, use a butter knife to gently loosen the cakes around the edges and tip the cakes out onto the racks to cool completely for about 15 minutes before assembling.

TO MAKE THE FROSTING

6. Break the chocolate into small pieces and place in a glass bowl. Microwave on high power for 1 minute. Stir, then heat in 15-second intervals until the chocolate is completely melted, stirring between each interval.

7. In a medium mixing bowl, using a handheld electric mixer on low speed, combine the powdered sugar, butter, shortening, ⅓ cup (80 ml) of milk, and vanilla bean paste. Mix for about 1 minute until combined. Increase the mixer speed to medium and mix for 2 minutes until smooth and slightly fluffy.

8. Reduce the mixer speed to low and slowly drizzle in the melted chocolate, mixing until combined. Increase the mixer speed to medium and beat for 2 minutes until fluffy and spreadable. If the frosting is too thick, add the remaining milk, 2 teaspoons at a time, until you reach your preferred consistency.

CONTINUED

Double-Chocolate Birthday Layer Cake CONTINUED

FOR THE FROSTING

6 ounces (180 grams)
unsweetened baking
chocolate

5 cups (600 grams)
powdered sugar, sifted

8 tablespoons
(1 stick; 112 grams)
dairy-free butter

¼ cup (48 grams)
shortening

⅓ to ½ cup (80 to 120 ml)
unsweetened
dairy-free milk

2 teaspoons vanilla bean
paste or vanilla extract

TO ASSEMBLE THE CAKE

9. Choose a cake stand or plate. Cut four parchment paper strips and arrange them around the edges. These will fit just under the edges of the cake, then be removed for a clean presentation once the cake is frosted.

10. Gently turn the first cake upside-down and place it on the stand so it sits in the center of the parchment strips. Remove the parchment circle from the bottom of the cake. Using an offset spatula or butter knife, spread ⅓ cup of frosting onto the top of the cake. Repeat with the second layer, then the third, with each cake layer stacked upside-down.

11. Frost the entire cake with a very thin layer of frosting, then decorate as you like. (I like to use a large star frosting tip to pipe loose swirls of frosting over the entire cake.)

12. Pull the parchment strips away from the cake. Serve immediately or refrigerate until ready to serve.

WHAT YOU NEED TO KNOW: Inverting the cakes before frosting is an easy way to create level layers without having to do any trimming.

MAKE IT NUT-FREE: Replace the almond meal with an equal amount of ground sunflower seed or ground sesame seed. Use a clean coffee grinder or high-speed blender to grind these, stopping when you have a fine crumbly texture. Don't grind too long or you'll have sunflower butter or tahini! You can also use the grinder to turn whole chia seeds into powder. Additionally, you can omit the coconut sugar and substitute 1 cup (220 grams) granulated sugar plus 1 cup (240) packed light brown sugar.

NEW YORK-STYLE CHEESECAKE

PREP TIME: 45 minutes, plus 8 hours 30 minutes to chill

BAKE TIME: 1 hour 20 minutes

MAKES 1 (9-INCH) CHEESECAKE

NUT-FREE

New York–style cheesecake is rich and silky. During Celiac Awareness Month, Aldi offers a cheesecake sampler and many who don't eat gluten run to stock up on it. If only they knew how easy it is to make one even more decadent at home! Don't wait for just one month out of the year to enjoy cheesecake.

FOR THE CRUST

Nonstick cooking spray

1½ cups (200 grams) gluten-free graham-style cracker crumbs

2 tablespoons (27.5 grams) granulated sugar

⅛ teaspoon fine sea salt

5 tablespoons (70 grams) unsalted butter, melted

FOR THE FILLING

5 (8-ounce; 240-gram) packages cream cheese, at room temperature

8 tablespoons (1 stick; 112 grams) unsalted butter, at room temperature

TO MAKE THE CRUST

1. Preheat the oven to 375°F. Coat the bottom and sides of a 9-inch springform pan with the cooking spray. Set aside.

2. In a medium mixing bowl, stir together the crumbs, sugar, and salt. Pour the melted butter over the crumb mixture and stir until well combined. Press the crust mixture into the bottom and 1 inch up the sides of the prepared pan.

3. Bake for 10 minutes until golden brown, then set on a wire rack to cool while you make the filling.

TO MAKE THE FILLING

4. In a large mixing bowl, using a handheld electric mixer on medium speed, combine the cream cheese, butter, and sour cream.

1 cup (240 grams)
  sour cream, at room
  temperature
1¾ cups (385 grams)
  granulated sugar
5 large eggs
2 large egg yolks
1 teaspoon vanilla bean
  paste or vanilla extract
1 teaspoon grated
  lemon zest

5. Add the sugar and mix to combine.

6. One at a time, add the eggs, mixing to combine after each. Do the same with the yolks. Mix in the vanilla bean paste and lemon zest.

7. Wrap the outside of the cooled springform pan with aluminum foil and place it in a large roasting pan. Pour the filling over the crust and place the roasting pan in the oven.

8. Carefully pour boiling water into the roasting pan to reach halfway up the sides of the springform pan, taking care not to splash any water into the filling. This creates a water bath, which is important for baking this cheesecake evenly and preventing cracks in the filling.

9. Bake for 1 hour 10 minutes to 1 hour 20 minutes, or until the center has only the slightest jiggle but is not completely set. Cool the cheesecake on a wire rack for about 30 minutes until the springform pan is cool enough to touch. Remove the foil and refrigerate for at least 8 hours before removing the springform ring and serving.

WHAT YOU NEED TO KNOW: When it's time to serve, cut the cheesecake with a hot knife, wiping it clean between each slice. To warm the knife, simply hold the blade under running hot water and dry it with a clean kitchen towel.

SALTED CARAMEL
APPLE TART **PAGE 110**

PIES, TARTS, AND FRUIT DESSERTS

PIECRUST

PREP TIME: 20 minutes, plus 1 hour to chill

MAKES 1 SINGLE OR 1 DOUBLE 9-INCH PIECRUST

DAIRY-FREE OPTION, EGG-FREE, NUT-FREE, VEGAN OPTION

I learned to make flaky, buttery piecrust in high school home economics class. Mrs. Anderson insisted we could learn to make a piecrust that was better than store-bought. She was right. It's even easier to make it without gluten because it doesn't get gummy if you have to roll your crust out more than once. The gluten-free flour lends itself naturally to the crunchy, flaky crust we all look forward to in a pie.

FOR A SINGLE PIECRUST (BOTTOM CRUST ONLY)

1½ cups (228 grams) Johnna's Favorite Gluten-Free All-Purpose Flour Blend (page 12)

1 tablespoon plus 2¼ teaspoons (24 grams) granulated sugar

½ teaspoon guar gum or xanthan gum

⅛ teaspoon fine sea salt

6 tablespoons (¾ stick; 84 grams) cold unsalted butter, cubed

TO MAKE EITHER A SINGLE OR DOUBLE PIECRUST

1. In a large mixing bowl, stir together the flour blend, sugar, guar gum, and salt to combine.

2. Add the cold butter to the flour mixture along with the shortening, and using a pastry blender or two forks, work the butter and shortening into the flour mixture until it feels crumbly with pea-size butter pieces.

3. Add the cold water to the flour mixture, and using the pastry blender or forks, mix until the crust comes together into a dry dough. If it's still very crumbly, mix in more cold water, 1 tablespoon at a time, until the dough is no longer crumbly. A small amount of liquid will pull it together quickly.

2 tablespoons (24 grams) shortening

¼ cup (60 ml) ice-cold water, plus more as needed

2½ cups (380 grams) Johnna's Favorite Gluten-Free All-Purpose Flour Blend (page 12)

3 tablespoons plus 1½ teaspoons (48 grams) granulated sugar

1 teaspoon guar gum or xanthan gum

¼ teaspoon fine sea salt

12 tablespoons (1½ sticks; 168 grams) cold unsalted butter, cubed

¼ cup (48 grams) shortening

½ cup (120 ml) ice-cold water, plus more as needed

4. Flatten the dough into a disk about 1 inch thick; if making a double crust, divide the dough into two pieces and flatten. Wrap the disk(s) in plastic and chill for at least 1 hour.

5. Remove one dough disk from the refrigerator and unwrap it. Spread the plastic wrap on a flat surface and place the dough in the center. Cover it with another large piece of plastic wrap. This makes it easy to roll out the piecrust without it sticking to your rolling pin and eliminates the need for additional flour. With a rolling pin, roll the dough into a 10-inch circle.

6. Remove the plastic wrap on top of the crust. Invert a pie pan onto the top of the piecrust, then flip over both the pie pan and crust. Gently press the piecrust into the pan and remove the plastic wrap. Finish the edges of the piecrust any way you like—I use a simple finishing method with thumb on one hand gently pushing out from the inside of the crust into thumb and index finger on the other to make a rippled edge—or simply trim the crust to fit your pan.

CONTINUED

7. If you are making a double crust, roll the second dough disk following step 5. Fill your pie and cover it with the top crust, then seal and trim or crimp together the edges of the two crusts as you like.

WHAT YOU NEED TO KNOW: This piecrust freezes well wrapped in plastic. When you are ready to use it, remove it from the freezer and thaw in the fridge for about 1 hour until it's just cool enough to roll out easily. I keep piecrust frozen year-round for quick quiches and hand pies.

VARIATION TIP: If you avoid refined sugar, or like a slightly less sweet crust, substitute 3 tablespoons (36 grams) coconut sugar for the granulated sugar. This will give your crust a bit more color as well, which is nice since gluten-free flour doesn't brown to the same golden color many expect in a piecrust.

MAKE IT VEGAN AND DAIRY-FREE: Replace the butter with an equal amount of dairy-free butter (such as Earth Balance).

STRAWBERRY GALETTE

PREP TIME: 30 minutes, plus 30 minutes to chill
BAKE TIME: 30 minutes, plus 15 minutes to cool

MAKES 1 (8-INCH) GALETTE
DAIRY-FREE OPTION,
EGG-FREE OPTION,
NUT-FREE, VEGAN OPTION,
WHOLE GRAIN

A galette is an easy way to become comfortable making pies. It is essentially a free-form pie baked on a baking sheet instead of in a pie pan. Beyond being less intimidating than making a traditional piecrust, a galette is a bit quicker and makes for an easy weeknight dessert.

FOR THE CRUST

1¼ cups (175 grams) Gluten-Free Whole-Grain Flour Blend (page 14)
1½ teaspoons granulated sugar or coconut sugar
½ teaspoon guar gum
¼ teaspoon salt
8 tablespoons (1 stick; 112 grams) cold unsalted butter, cubed
6 to 8 tablespoons (90 to 120 ml) ice-cold water

TO MAKE THE CRUST

1. In a large mixing bowl, whisk together the flour blend, granulated sugar, guar gum, and salt to combine.

2. Using a pastry blender or fork, cut the butter cubes into the flour mixture until you have pea-size pieces. Add 6 tablespoons (90 ml) of the ice-cold water and mix to incorporate. Mix in more water, 1 tablespoon at a time, until the dough comes together. Form the dough into a disk, wrap it in plastic wrap, and refrigerate for 30 minutes.

3. Preheat the oven to 350°F.

CONTINUED

FOR THE FILLING

2½ cups (450 grams) sliced
strawberries

¼ cup (55 grams)
granulated sugar plus
1½ teaspoons granulated
sugar or demerara sugar

1 teaspoon vanilla bean
paste or vanilla extract

1 large egg white

1 tablespoon water

4. Remove the dough from the refrigerator and unwrap it. Spread the plastic wrap on a flat surface and place the dough in the center. Cover it with another large piece of plastic wrap. This makes it easy to roll out the piecrust without it sticking to your rolling pin and eliminates the need for additional flour. With a rolling pin, roll the dough into a 10-inch circle.

5. Remove the top piece of plastic from the dough and replace it with a piece of parchment paper. Slowly invert the crust and slide it onto a baking sheet, then remove the remaining plastic wrap. Set aside.

TO MAKE THE FILLING

6. In a medium mixing bowl, combine the strawberries, ¼ cup (55 grams) sugar, and vanilla. Toss to coat.

7. Arrange the strawberries in a single layer on the crust, leaving a 2-inch border all the way around. Carefully fold 2-inch sections of the crust up and over the edge of the filling all the way around, pleating the dough where it folds.

8. In a small bowl, whisk together the egg white and water until frothy. Using a pastry brush, coat the folded crust with the egg white, then sprinkle the remaining 1½ teaspoons of sugar over the top of the crust.

9. Bake for 26 to 30 minutes, or until the crust is golden brown and the filling is bubbling. Cool on the baking sheet for at least 15 minutes before slicing.

MAKE IT DAIRY-FREE: Substitute an equal amount of dairy-free butter (such as Earth Balance).

MAKE IT EGG-FREE: Instead of using an egg white and water for the egg wash, use 2 tablespoons (30 ml) unsweetened almond milk, if nuts are not an issue, to brush the crust.

MAKE IT VEGAN: Follow both of the preceding Make It Dairy-Free and Make It Egg-Free tips.

VARIATION TIP: Drizzle each slice of galette with aged balsamic vinegar or balsamic vinegar glaze (I recommend Roland or Trader Joe's brand) immediately before serving. It's lovely with the strawberries!

RASPBERRY HAND PIES

These hand pies are the perfect size for an on-the-go or lunchbox treat—a bit of pie without committing to an entire piece. Use large cookie cutters to turn them into fun shapes. I sometimes make them in seasonal shapes, like Christmas trees, hearts for Valentine's Day, and stars for the Fourth of July. I always enjoy making pie with kiddos, but the small size of these hand pies is particularly well-suited to baking with children.

PREP TIME: 1 hour
BAKE TIME: 20 minutes, plus 25 minutes to cool

MAKES 12 HAND PIES
DAIRY-FREE OPTION,
EGG-FREE OPTION,
NUT-FREE, VEGAN OPTION

2 cups (246 grams) fresh raspberries

¼ cup (55 grams) granulated sugar or (48 grams) coconut sugar

1 tablespoon plus 1 teaspoon (10.5 grams) arrowroot

1 teaspoon freshly squeezed lemon juice

½ teaspoon grated lemon zest

1 double Piecrust (page 92), prepared according to the directions

1 large egg white

1 tablespoon water

1. Preheat the oven to 400°F. Line two baking sheets with parchment paper and set aside.

2. In a medium mixing bowl, combine the raspberries, sugar, arrowroot, lemon juice, and lemon zest. Toss until well coated.

3. Remove one dough disk from the refrigerator and roll it out per the instructions on page 93. Use a 3-inch cookie cutter shape of your choosing to cut 12 shapes. Transfer the shapes to the prepared baking sheets, spacing them 1 inch apart. Repeat with the second dough disk, cutting the same number and shape of crusts. Leave these on your work surface.

4. In the middle of the piecrusts on the baking sheet, place 1 heaping tablespoon of the berry mixture.

5. In a small bowl, whisk the egg white and water until frothy. Using a pastry brush, coat the edges of the piecrusts around the filling. Place the remaining piecrust shapes over the filling and use a fork to seal the edges. Using a sharp knife, cut a small X in the top of each hand pie for ventilation. Brush the tops with the egg wash.

6. Bake for 18 to 20 minutes, or until the piecrusts are golden brown. Cool on the baking sheets for 10 minutes, then transfer the pies to a wire rack to cool completely for about 15 minutes before enjoying.

WHAT YOU NEED TO KNOW: This recipe works well with most fruits in the same quantity, such as apples, blackberries, blueberries, peaches, and strawberries. Cut larger fruits into small enough pieces to easily fit in a small pie.

MAKE IT DAIRY-FREE: See Piecrust, Make It Vegan and Dairy-Free tip (page 94).

MAKE IT EGG-FREE: Replace the egg wash with ¼ cup unsweetened almond milk, if nuts are not an issue.

MAKE IT VEGAN: Follow both of the preceding Make It Dairy-Free and Make It Egg-Free tips.

COCONUT CREAM PIE

PREP TIME: 1 hour, plus
8 hours to chill
BAKE TIME: 22 minutes

MAKES 1 (9-INCH) PIE

If you ever watched Gilligan's Island, *you surely noticed the only dessert they ever had was coconut cream pie, usually made by Mary Ann. The pie always ended up smashed in someone's face through a series of shenanigans. Because of this TV show, I often asked for coconut cream pie. Then, I learned to make it myself. It's far too good to smash in someone's face, though. It's best enjoyed by the slice with a fork instead.*

FOR THE PIE

1 single Piecrust (page 92),
   prepared according to
   the directions
4 large egg yolks
1 large egg white
3 tablespoons (24 grams)
   arrowroot
1 (13.5 ounce; 399 ml) can
   full-fat coconut milk
1 cup (240 ml) half-and-half
⅔ cup (147 grams)
   granulated sugar
¼ teaspoon fine sea salt

TO MAKE THE PIE

1. Preheat the oven to 350°F.

2. Roll out the piecrust and place it in a 9-inch pie pan. Cover with aluminum foil and fill with 1 pound dried beans or pie weights.

3. Bake for 10 minutes. This is call blind baking (see What You Need to Know, page 102). Remove the beans and foil (let the beans cool, then store in an airtight jar to use for your next piecrust). Bake the crust for 10 to 12 minutes more, or until golden brown. Place on a wire rack to cool while you make the filling.

4. In a small bowl, whisk together the egg yolks, egg white, and arrowroot to blend. Set aside.

1 cup (80 grams)
sweetened shredded
coconut

2 tablespoons (28 grams)
unsalted butter, at room
temperature

1 teaspoon vanilla bean
paste or vanilla extract

FOR THE TOPPING

2 cups (480 ml) heavy
(whipping) cream

⅓ cup (73 grams)
granulated sugar

1½ teaspoons vanilla bean
paste or vanilla extract

2 to 3 tablespoons
(15 to 22.5 grams)
sweetened
shredded coconut

5. In a medium saucepan over medium heat, combine the coconut milk, half-and-half, sugar, and salt. Bring to a boil, then reduce the heat to medium-low and cook for about 2 minutes, or until the liquid returns to a boil.

6. While whisking continually to prevent the eggs from scrambling, carefully stream ½ cup of the heated milk mixture into the eggs. Pour the egg mixture into the saucepan and cook for about 2 minutes, undisturbed, or until the mixture flows off the whisk in wide ribbons.

7. Remove the filling mixture from the heat and stir in the coconut, butter, and vanilla bean paste until the butter melts and everything is well combined. Pour the pudding into the pie-crust. Cover the pie tightly with plastic wrap, making sure the plastic touches the filling to prevent it from forming a skin. Refrigerate the pie overnight.

TO MAKE THE TOPPING

8. In a medium bowl, using a handheld electric mixer on high speed, whip the heavy cream, sugar, and vanilla bean paste for 3 to 4 minutes until light and fluffy. Spread or pipe the whipped cream over the pie.

CONTINUED

9. In a small skillet over medium-low heat, toast the coconut for 4 to 5 minutes, stirring frequently, until it is a golden-brown color. Cool for 5 minutes before sprinkling the coconut over the whipped cream.

WHAT YOU NEED TO KNOW: This recipe uses both coconut milk and half-and-half–don't skip it! The coconut milk adds depth to the filling's coconut flavor that's missing using only half-and-half.

WHAT YOU NEED TO KNOW: Blind baking is baking a piecrust before it is filled, usually for pies that contain a filling that bakes for less time than the crust, or very wet fillings that could make the crust soggy. Placing pie weights or dried beans in the crust while baking keeps the bottom from bubbling and the sides from slouching.

PUMPKIN PIE

PREP TIME: 1 hour
BAKE TIME: 1 hour, plus
2 hours to cool

MAKES 1 (9-INCH) PIE
NUT-FREE

The first pie I baked after going gluten-free was a pumpkin pie for Thanksgiving dinner. Friends joined us for our meal that year and the entire pie was quickly devoured. If you aren't reassured by now that you can create traditional desserts that no one will know are gluten-free, consider this proof!

1 single Piecrust (page 92), prepared according to the directions
¾ cup (165 grams) granulated sugar
1½ teaspoons pumpkin pie spice
½ teaspoon fine sea salt
1 (15-ounce; 450-gram) can pure pumpkin puree (not pie filling)
1½ cups (360 ml) evaporated milk
2 large eggs

1. Preheat the oven to 425°F.

2. Roll out the piecrust and place it in a 9-inch pie pan.

3. In a large mixing bowl, whisk together the sugar, pumpkin pie spice, and salt to combine. Add the pumpkin puree, milk, and eggs. Whisk well to combine. Pour the filling into the crust.

4. Bake for 15 minutes, then reduce the oven temperature to 350°F and bake for 35 to 45 minutes, or until a knife inserted into the center of the pie comes out clean. Cool on a wire rack for at least 2 hours before slicing.

WHAT YOU NEED TO KNOW: Glass pie pans may cook a bit faster than the metal variety.

PEACH COBBLER

PREP TIME: 30 minutes
BAKE TIME: 45 minutes

MAKES 1 (9-INCH) COBBLER
DAIRY-FREE OPTION,
NUT-FREE

Peach cobbler is the ultimate comfort food to me. Where I live, peach orchards are plentiful and visiting them during the summer was a family tradition. Sometimes my dad would even churn homemade peach ice cream, a process that seemed to take all day. Thankfully, cobbler is quicker to make and equally as delicious. You can make it year-round with fresh or frozen sliced peaches.

Nonstick cooking spray
1 cup (152 grams) Johnna's
   Favorite Gluten-Free
   All-Purpose Flour Blend
   (page 12)
¾ cup (165 grams)
   granulated sugar, divided
1½ teaspoons
   baking powder
⅛ teaspoon fine sea salt
1 cup (240 ml) whole milk
1 large egg
3 cups (462 grams) sliced
   peaches, fresh or frozen
   and thawed
1 tablespoon freshly
   squeezed lemon juice
½ teaspoon ground
   cinnamon

1. Preheat the oven to 350°F. Coat a 9-inch square baking pan with cooking spray. Set aside.

2. In a medium mixing bowl, whisk together the flour blend, ½ cup (110 grams) of sugar, the baking powder, and salt to combine. Add the milk and egg and stir to combine.

3. In another medium mixing bowl, toss the peaches with the remaining ¼ cup (55 grams) of sugar, the lemon juice, and cinnamon until well coated.

4. Pour the batter into the bottom of the prepared pan and top with the peaches. Bake for 40 to 45 minutes, or until a toothpick inserted into the center of the cobbler comes out clean. Serve warm.

WHAT YOU NEED TO KNOW: If using frozen peaches, or particularly juicy fresh peaches, let them drain for 10 minutes in a colander over the sink before adding them to the cobbler.

MAKE IT DAIRY-FREE: Substitute an equal amount of dairy-free unsweetened milk (such as almond, soy, or hemp) of your choice.

CHERRY FRUIT CRISP

PREP TIME: 30 minutes
BAKE TIME: 40 minutes, plus 15 minutes to cool

MAKES 1 (9-INCH) CRISP
DAIRY-FREE OPTION, EGG-FREE, NUT-FREE, VEGAN OPTION, WHOLE GRAIN

This fruit crisp has a streusel topping that comes together in just a few short minutes, making it perfect for an impromptu dessert. While this recipe features cherries, try it with other fruits, such as strawberries, peaches, or apples.

FOR THE STREUSEL TOPPING

Nonstick cooking spray
1½ cups (126 grams) Purity Protocol certified gluten-free oats
¾ cup (180 grams) packed light brown sugar
½ cup (70 grams) Gluten-Free Whole-Grain Flour Blend (page 14)
1 teaspoon ground cinnamon
¼ teaspoon ground nutmeg
⅛ teaspoon fine sea salt
8 tablespoons (1 stick; 112 grams) cold unsalted butter, cubed

1. Preheat the oven to 350°F. Coat a 9-inch square baking pan with cooking spray. Set aside.

TO MAKE THE STREUSEL TOPPING

2. In a large mixing bowl, stir together the oats, light brown sugar, flour blend, cinnamon, nutmeg, and salt. Using a pastry cutter or fork, cut the butter into the dry mixture until crumbly.

TO MAKE THE FILLING

3. In a medium mixing bowl, toss the cherries with the flour blend and granulated sugar to coat. Pour the fruit into the prepared pan.

4. Drop the streusel topping over the cherries in large dollops.

FOR THE FILLING

5 cups (about 2 pounds;
908 grams) pitted fresh or
frozen cherries

2 tablespoons (18 grams)
Gluten-Free Whole-Grain
Flour Blend (page 14)

¾ cup (165 grams)
granulated sugar

5. Bake for 35 to 40 minutes, or until the topping is browned and the filling is bubbling. Place the pan on a wire rack to cool for 15 minutes before serving warm.

MAKE IT DAIRY-FREE AND VEGAN: Substitute an equal amount of dairy-free butter (such as Earth Balance).

LEMON TART

PREP TIME: 45 minutes, plus 3 hours 30 minutes to chill
BAKE TIME: 35 minutes

MAKES 1 (9-INCH) TART

NUT-FREE

Tarts have such a classy, elegant appearance. If you use a fluted tart pan with a removable bottom, all you have to do is pat the crust in—no rolling required. The filling is a no-bake curd, which means you don't have to worry about it curdling or not setting up in your beautiful tart crust. Don't you just love a fancy dessert that is also easy to make?

FOR THE TART CRUST

1 cup (2 sticks; 224 grams) unsalted butter, at room temperature
½ cup (110 grams) granulated sugar
1 large egg yolk
1½ teaspoons whole milk
2½ cups (380 grams) Johnna's Favorite Gluten-Free All-Purpose Flour Blend (page 12)
1 teaspoon xanthan gum
¼ teaspoon fine sea salt
Nonstick cooking spray

TO MAKE THE TART CRUST

1. In a medium mixing bowl, using a handheld electric mixer on medium speed, combine the butter and sugar until smooth. Add the egg yolk and milk, mixing to combine.

2. In a small bowl, whisk together the flour blend, xanthan gum, and salt. Add half the dry mixture to the wet ingredients, mixing on low speed until just combined. Repeat with the remaining flour mixture until you have a wet, loose dough. Gather the dough into a ball and wrap it with a large piece of plastic wrap. Flatten into a 9-inch disk and refrigerate for 30 minutes.

3. While the dough chills, preheat the oven to 375°F. Coat a 9-inch fluted tart pan with cooking spray.

4. Remove the dough from the refrigerator and use your hands to gently pat it into the tart pan in an even thickness.

FOR THE FILLING

4 large eggs

4 large egg yolks

1 cup (220 grams)
  granulated sugar

1 cup (240 ml) freshly
  squeezed lemon juice

⅛ teaspoon fine sea salt

8 tablespoons plus
  2 tablespoons (1¼ sticks;
  140 grams) unsalted
  butter, cubed

5. Bake for 15 minutes. Prick the crust all over with a fork. Bake for about 20 minutes more, or until just golden brown. Place on a wire rack to cool while you make the filling.

TO MAKE THE FILLING

6. Set a fine-mesh strainer in a large bowl and place it near the stovetop.

7. In a large saucepan over medium heat, combine the eggs, egg yolks, sugar, lemon juice, and salt. Whisk until smooth. Cook for 3 to 4 minutes, stirring constantly, until the mixture has the thickness of gravy. Remove from the heat and add the butter, a few cubes at a time, whisking until well incorporated after each addition.

8. Pass the filling through the strainer into the bowl. Pour the filling into the cooled crust and refrigerate for about 3 hours, or until set.

9. Remove the fluted ring from the pan and cut the tart into wedges to serve.

WHAT YOU NEED TO KNOW: Plan to make this tart during Meyer lemon season. Meyer lemons are much sweeter than standard lemons, yet have that wonderful lemon flavor with just the right tartness.

SALTED CARAMEL APPLE TART

PREP TIME: 1 hour
30 minutes
BAKE TIME: 55 minutes,
plus at least 10 minutes to
cool

MAKES 1 (9-INCH) TART
NUT-FREE

The combination of salty and sweet makes it hard to eat just one slice of this tart. I've included instructions on making salted caramel sauce, which isn't just for this tart! Use it to top ice cream or brownies, or stir a spoonful into your hot cocoa or coffee.

FOR THE TART

1 tart crust (see Lemon
   Tart, page 108)
5 cups (550 grams)
   sliced unpeeled Granny
   Smith apples (about
   3 large apples)
¼ cup (60 grams) packed
   light brown sugar
2 tablespoons (19 grams)
   Johnna's Favorite
   Gluten-Free All-Purpose
   Flour Blend (page 12)
1 teaspoon ground
   cinnamon
¼ teaspoon
   ground nutmeg

TO MAKE THE TART

1. Prepare the tart crust per the directions on page 108, stopping after you bake the crust for the first 15 minutes. Place on a wire rack to cool for 15 minutes while you prepare the filling.

2. In a large mixing bowl, combine the apples, light brown sugar, flour blend, cinnamon, and nutmeg. Toss well to coat the apples. Arrange the slices evenly over the tart crust. Pour any remaining mixture over the apples.

3. Bake for 35 to 40 minutes, or until the apples are soft when pierced with a fork and the crust is starting to pull away from the edges of the pan. Place on a wire rack to cool for at least 10 minutes or until completely cool before removing the fluted ring and slicing.

½ cup (110 grams)
granulated sugar
3 tablespoons (42 grams)
unsalted butter, cubed
¼ cup (60 ml) heavy
(whipping) cream
½ teaspoon fine sea salt

TO MAKE THE SALTED CARAMEL

4. While the tart bakes, place the granulated sugar in a small saucepan over medium heat. Cook for 5 to 6 minutes, stirring constantly, or until the sugar becomes clumpy.

5. Continue to cook until the sugar is completely melted, then stir in the butter until it melts. Cook for about 2 minutes, undisturbed, until bubbling.

6. Slowly stir in the heavy cream. The caramel will bubble up. Once the cream is incorporated, boil for 1 minute. Keep a close eye on this, as it will rise in the pan.

7. Remove from the heat and stir in the salt. Let cool in the pan until the tart is ready to serve.

8. Slice the tart into wedges and drizzle with the caramel just before serving. Refrigerate any leftover caramel sauce in a sealed jar.

WHAT YOU NEED TO KNOW: Granny Smith apples are my preferred apple for pies and tarts. They are among the firmer varieties of apple and don't become overly soft when baking. Available year-round, they're more affordable than other types of apples, but if you can afford a splurge, Honeycrisp apples are also very nice in this tart.

CHALLAH
PAGE 119

BREADS AND CRACKERS

YEASTED SANDWICH LOAF

PREP TIME: 1 hour
15 minutes
BAKE TIME: 42 minutes,
plus 1 hour 15 minutes to
cool

MAKES 1 (9-INCH) LOAF
DAIRY-FREE OPTION,
NUT-FREE

For many of us, finding a store-bought loaf of gluten-free bread similar in size, texture, and flavor to the bread we like to make sandwiches with can be a challenge, not to mention more expensive. When creating this recipe, my goal was a loaf of bread that is sliceable and sturdy without being gummy, doesn't need to be toasted to be flavorful, and is large enough to make a filling sandwich. Whether for peanut butter and jelly, grilled cheese, or a pile of deli favorites, this bread is up to the task.

Nonstick cooking spray

3 cups (405 grams)
   Gluten-Free Bread Flour
   Blend (page 13)

2 tablespoons (27.5 grams)
   granulated sugar

1 (2.5-ounce; 7-gram)
   packet instant yeast

1 teaspoon fine sea salt

1 teaspoon xanthan gum

1 teaspoon psyllium
   husk powder

¼ teaspoon cream of tartar

1. Spray a 9-by-5-inch loaf pan with cooking spray. Set aside.

2. In a large mixing bowl, using a handheld electric mixer on low speed, combine the flour blend, sugar, yeast, salt, xanthan gum, psyllium husk powder, and cream of tartar until combined.

3. Add the milk and oil, mixing on low speed until combined. Increase the mixer speed to medium and, one at a time, add the eggs, mixing after each addition. Add the egg white and mix to combine. Continue mixing on medium speed for 3 minutes until the dough is smooth. Transfer the dough to the prepared loaf pan. Cover with a damp kitchen towel and let rise in a warm area for 1 hour until visibly larger.

1 cup (240 ml) whole milk,
  warmed to 95°F
¼ cup (60 ml) grapeseed oil
  or vegetable oil
2 large eggs
1 large egg white

4. During the last 10 minutes of rising, preheat the oven to 350°F.

5. Bake for 38 to 42 minutes, or until browned on top and the internal temperature tested with a thermometer reaches 190°F. Cool the bread in the pan for 15 minutes, then use a knife to gently release the edges and turn the loaf out onto a wire rack to cool completely for 1 hour before slicing.

WHAT YOU NEED TO KNOW: If you are looking for a traditional, rectangular loaf of sandwich bread, bake this recipe in an 8-inch Pullman pan with a lid. Spray the inside of the pan's lid and follow the recipe through step 4, letting the dough rise with the lid on the pan instead of using a damp towel. Bake for 35 minutes, remove the lid, and bake for 3 to 7 minutes more, or until the top browns. Remove and cool as directed.

MAKE IT DAIRY-FREE: Use an equal amount of unsweetened dairy-free milk (such as almond, soy, or hemp) to replace the whole milk.

ARTISAN BOULE

PREP TIME: 30 minutes, plus 1 hour to rise
BAKE TIME: 40 minutes, plus 1 hour 15 minutes to cool

MAKES 1 (8-INCH) ROUND LOAF

DAIRY-FREE OPTION, NUT-FREE, WHOLE GRAIN

This classic round loaf will remind you of those crusty bakery versions. It has a golden-brown crust, a tender crumb, and is shaped by hand with no kneading required. I like to serve this bread on cold nights with creamy potato soup or chowder.

1½ cups (360 ml) whole milk, warmed to 95°F

2 tablespoons (27.5 grams) plus 1 teaspoon granulated sugar, divided

1 (2.5-ounce; 7-gram) packet active dry yeast

¼ cup (60 ml) plus 1 tablespoon grapeseed oil or vegetable oil, divided

1 tablespoon apple cider vinegar

2 large eggs

3¼ cups (455 grams) Gluten-Free Whole-Grain Flour Blend (page 14), plus 2 tablespoons (18 grams) for dusting

1. In a large mixing bowl, stir together the milk, 1 teaspoon of sugar, and the yeast just to combine. Let sit for 10 minutes to bloom the yeast (it will bubble lightly). Whisk in ¼ cup (60 ml) of oil, the vinegar, and eggs to combine.

2. In a medium mixing bowl, stir together 3¼ cups (455 grams) of flour blend, the remaining 2 tablespoons (27.5 grams) of sugar, the psyllium husk powder, xanthan gum, baking powder, baking soda, salt, and cream of tartar.

3. Using a wooden spoon, slowly incorporate the flour mixture into the wet mixture. Mix for about 3 minutes, or until all ingredients are well combined and you have a wet dough.

4. Coat a small (4-cup, 960-ml) mixing bowl with cooking spray. Set aside.

1 tablespoon psyllium
   husk powder
2 teaspoons xanthan gum
2 teaspoons baking powder
1 teaspoon baking soda
1 teaspoon sea salt
½ teaspoon cream of tartar
Nonstick cooking spray
5 ice cubes

5. Place a large piece of parchment paper, about 12 by 16 inches, on a work surface and sprinkle it with the remaining 2 tablespoons (18 grams) of flour blend. Turn the dough out onto the floured parchment and shape it into an 8-inch round loaf, turning to coat all sides in the flour. Gently transfer the loaf to the prepared bowl. Cover with a damp kitchen towel and place in a warm area for 1 hour to rise. The bread should completely fill the 4-cup (960-ml) bowl, rising just over the top.

6. During the last 10 minutes of rising, preheat the oven to 350°F and line a baking sheet with parchment paper.

7. Gently turn the bread out onto the prepared baking sheet. Using a paring knife, make a 3-inch X on top of the loaf. Using a pastry brush, coat the loaf with the remaining 1 tablespoon of oil.

8. Place the ice cubes into a small cast-iron or other oven-safe skillet and set it on the bottom rack of the oven. Place the baking sheet with the bread on the rack above. (The ice helps keep moisture in the bread and creates a crust.)

CONTINUED

9. Bake for 35 to 40 minutes, or until the loaf has an evenly browned crust and the internal temperature tested with a thermometer reaches 185°F.

10. Cool on the sheet for 15 minutes, then transfer to a wire rack to cool completely for 1 hour before slicing.

WHAT YOU NEED TO KNOW: This is a sturdy loaf of bread, which makes it ideal to use as a vessel for a hearty soup or dip. Hollow out the center, saving the removed bread to eat or toast into croutons.

MAKE IT DAIRY-FREE: Use an equal amount of unsweetened dairy-free milk (such as almond, soy, or hemp) to replace the whole milk.

CHALLAH

PREP TIME: 2 hours
30 minutes
BAKE TIME: 42 minutes,
plus 15 minutes to cool

MAKES 1 (9-INCH) LOAF
DAIRY-FREE, NUT-FREE

Every Friday, my friend shares beautiful photos on social media of the challah she baked that week for Shabbat. I long envied her beautifully braided loaves, but found it wasn't an easy bread to make without gluten. It took persistence to create a recipe for challah that is both gluten-free and can be braided, plus is soft and delicious. After much trial, here is my easy recipe that works well braided or baked in a challah mold.

2 cups (270 grams)
Gluten-Free Bread Flour
Blend (page 13), divided

½ cup (110 grams)
granulated sugar

2 (2.5-ounce; 7-gram)
packets instant yeast

1 tablespoon psyllium
husk powder

1 teaspoon xanthan gum

1 teaspoon baking powder

½ teaspoon salt

⅔ cup (160 ml) plus
1 tablespoon
water, divided

1. In a large mixing bowl, using a handheld electric mixer on low speed, mix 1¾ cups (236.25 grams) of flour blend, the sugar, yeast, psyllium husk powder, xanthan gum, baking powder, and salt until combined.

2. Add ⅔ cup (160 ml) of water and the oil and mix until combined.

3. Add 1 egg and the egg yolk, mixing until well combined. Increase the mixer speed to medium and mix for about 5 minutes, until the dough is smooth.

CONTINUED

¼ cup (60 ml) grapeseed oil
  or vegetable oil
2 large eggs
1 large egg yolk
Nonstick cooking spray
  (optional)

4. **If braiding the dough:** Place a large piece of parchment paper, about 12 by 16 inches, on a work surface and dust it with the remaining ¼ cup (33.75 grams) of flour blend. Transfer the dough to the parchment and divide into three even pieces. Use your hands to shape each piece into a log, then roll the ropes into 12-inch strips. Braid the dough strips using a simple three-strand braid. Gently tuck both ends under, making sure the loaf is slightly shorter than 9 inches long. Transfer the dough and parchment into a 9-by-5-inch loaf pan and cover with a damp kitchen towel. Let rise in a warm area for about 2 hours, or until the dough has risen by about 50 percent.

5. **If using a challah mold:** Generously coat your mold with the cooking spray. Place the dough into the mold and cover with a damp kitchen towel. Let rise in a warm area for about 2 hours, or until the dough has doubled in size and completely fills the mold.

6. During the last 10 minutes of rising, preheat the oven to 325°F.

7. In a small bowl, whisk the remaining egg with the remaining 1 tablespoon of water for an egg wash.

8. **If your loaf is braided:** Brush the loaf with the egg wash. Bake for 20 minutes, then brush again with egg wash. Bake for 20 to 22 minutes more, or until the bread is evenly browned on top and the internal temperature tested with a thermometer reaches 185°F.

9. **If your loaf is in a challah mold:** Bake for 30 minutes. Remove the loaf from the oven. Place a baking sheet on top of the mold and gently invert it, removing the loaf from the pan onto the baking sheet. Brush the loaf with the egg wash and bake for 5 minutes. Remove from the oven and brush again with the egg wash. Bake for 5 to 7 minutes more, or until the egg wash no longer looks wet.

10. Cool the loaf on the pan for 15 minutes before transferring to a wire rack. This bread may be enjoyed warm if pulled apart in pieces. It slices best after cooling for 30 minutes or more.

WHAT YOU NEED TO KNOW: Challah makes amazing French toast. Although it is hard to have leftovers because it is so good, it is worth making a second loaf to save, especially for French toast. It's also well suited to bread pudding and strata.

VARIATION TIP: To make honey challah, instead of ½ cup (110 grams) granulated sugar, use 2 tablespoons (40 grams) honey and 2 tablespoons (27.5 grams) granulated sugar.

RUSTIC HERBED CRACKERS

PREP TIME: 20 minutes, plus 30 minutes to chill
BAKE TIME: 17 minutes, plus 15 minutes to cool

MAKES 48 CRACKERS

DAIRY-FREE OPTION, EGG-FREE, NUT-FREE, VEGAN OPTION, WHOLE GRAIN

Homemade crackers are easy to make and so versatile. Switch up the herbs in this recipe to suit your fancy. I most often use an Italian herb blend with oregano, basil, marjoram, rosemary, and thyme.

1 cup (140 grams) Gluten-Free Whole-Grain Flour Blend (page 14)

1 teaspoon dried herbs or 1 tablespoon fresh herbs of choice, finely chopped

½ teaspoon xanthan gum

½ teaspoon baking powder

½ teaspoon granulated sugar

¼ teaspoon fine sea salt

4 tablespoons (½ stick; 56 grams) cold unsalted butter, cubed

¼ cup (60 ml) ice-cold water

1. In a medium mixing bowl, whisk the flour blend, herbs, xanthan gum, baking powder, sugar, and salt to combine.

2. Using a pastry cutter or two forks, work the butter into the mixture until it is crumbly, and you have pea-size butter pieces.

3. Add the cold water, 1 tablespoon at a time, mixing after each addition, until a soft dough forms. You may find it pulls together perfectly with 3 tablespoons (45 ml) and just a couple more drops of water, or it may take the entire ¼ cup (60 ml). Form the dough into a disk, wrap with plastic wrap, and refrigerate for 30 minutes.

4. Preheat the oven to 400°F. Line two baking sheets with parchment paper.

5. Remove the dough from the refrigerator. Unwrap the plastic and spread it on a work surface. Place the dough on top and lay another piece of plastic on the dough. Using a rolling pin, roll the dough into a 12-by-6-inch rectangle, ⅛ inch thick. Using a knife or pizza cutter, cut the dough into 1½-inch squares. Place the squares on the prepared baking sheets ½ inch apart.

6. Bake for 15 to 17 minutes, or until the crackers are light brown on the underside. It may be tempting to bake them longer, but these crackers will go from done to burnt in a flash, so keep a close eye on them. Remove from the oven and cool on the baking sheets for 15 minutes before eating.

WHAT YOU NEED TO KNOW: Not all dried spices or spice blends are gluten-free. When choosing packaged herbs, read the ingredient labels closely and contact the manufacturer if it isn't clear if the spices are gluten-free. I use Penzeys spices for the peace of mind that their blends don't contain any anti-caking ingredients with gluten.

MAKE IT DAIRY-FREE AND VEGAN: Replace the butter with an equal amount of dairy-free butter (such as Earth Balance).

CRISPY BUTTER CRACKERS

When I could eat gluten, I used butter crackers in so many ways beyond snacking. One of my favorite appetizers was pimiento cheese spread on a Ritz cracker and popped under the broiler briefly. I would crumble crackers over broccoli-cheese casserole or spread peanut butter between two crackers and then dip them in chocolate. I'd even use the crumbs at the bottom of a box in place of bread crumbs to make veggie burgers. This recipe creates crackers that are just as delicious and versatile as Ritz, and you can enjoy them fresh from the oven.

PREP TIME: 30 minutes, plus 30 minutes to chill
BAKE TIME: 8 minutes, plus 30 minutes to cool

MAKES 36 CRACKERS

DAIRY-FREE OPTION, EGG-FREE, NUT-FREE, VEGAN OPTION

2 cups (270 grams) Gluten-Free Bread Flour Blend (page 13)

1 tablespoon baking powder

2 teaspoons granulated sugar

1 teaspoon fine sea salt, divided

1 teaspoon xanthan gum

6 tablespoons (¾ stick; 84 grams) cold unsalted butter, cubed

1. In a large mixing bowl, whisk together the flour blend, baking powder, sugar, ½ teaspoon of salt, and the xanthan gum to combine.

2. Add the cubed butter. Using a pastry cutter or two forks, cut the butter into the flour mixture until you have pea-size butter pieces. Drizzle in the oil and mix to combine.

3. Add ⅓ cup (80 ml) of cold water and mix to pull together a dough. Mix in more water, 1 tablespoon at a time, until the dough holds together but is not sticky. Wrap the dough in plastic wrap and refrigerate for 30 minutes.

4. Preheat the oven to 400°F. Line two baking sheets with parchment paper.

2 tablespoons (30 ml)
  grapeseed oil or
  vegetable oil
⅓ cup (80 ml) plus 1 to
  2 tablespoons
  (15 to 30 ml)
  ice-cold water
2 tablespoons (30 ml)
  melted unsalted butter

5. Remove the dough from the refrigerator and divide into two equal portions. Place one portion on top of a large piece of plastic wrap and cover with another piece of plastic wrap. Using a rolling pin, roll the dough to ⅛-inch thickness. Using a 1½-inch round cutter, cut out the crackers, then place them on the prepared baking sheets. Repeat with the second portion of the dough, re-rolling the scraps to cut more crackers.

6. Using a pastry brush, brush the crackers with the melted butter and sprinkle with the remaining ½ teaspoon of salt. Use a toothpick to poke 4 or 5 holes into each cracker.

7. Bake for 7 to 8 minutes, or until lightly browned. Cool on the baking sheets for 15 minutes, then move to a wire rack to cool for 15 minutes more, or until completely cooled. The crackers will not be crisp until they have cooled.

WHAT YOU NEED TO KNOW: These crackers are pretty cut with a round, fluted cutter. This is the shape you are familiar with. These cutters are available in a nested set for under $10.

MAKE IT DAIRY-FREE AND VEGAN: Replace the butter with an equal amount of a dairy-free butter (such as Earth Balance).

CHEESE STRAWS

Cheese straws have a permanent spot on my grazing boards and charcuterie platters. I like to stand them in a wide-mouth Mason jar and place the jar directly on the platter. I also like to serve these with wine and cocktails. But my favorite? Broken into bite-size pieces and sprinkled over a bowl of tomato soup.

PREP TIME: 30 minutes
BAKE TIME: 20 minutes, plus 50 minutes to cool

MAKES 24 STRAWS
EGG-FREE, NUT-FREE

8 tablespoons (1 stick; 112 grams) unsalted butter, at room temperature

2 cups (160 grams) shredded sharp Cheddar cheese

1¼ cups (190 grams) plus 2 tablespoons (19 grams) Johnna's Favorite Gluten-Free All-Purpose Flour Blend (page 12), divided

½ teaspoon xanthan gum

½ teaspoon fine sea salt

⅛ to ¼ teaspoon cayenne pepper

1. Preheat the oven to 350°F. Line two baking sheets with parchment paper.

2. In a large mixing bowl, using a handheld electric mixer on medium speed, beat the butter until fluffy. Add the cheese and mix for 2 to 3 minutes until the mixture is smooth.

3. Add 1¼ cups (190 grams) of flour blend, the xanthan gum, salt, and cayenne pepper to taste. Mix on medium speed just until the mixture pulls together into a dough.

CONTINUED

4. Sprinkle the remaining 2 tablespoons (19 grams) of flour blend onto a work surface or large piece of parchment. Place the dough on top and use a rolling pin to roll it into a 6-by-12-inch rectangle. Using a knife or pizza cutter, cut the dough into 24 strips. Transfer the strips to the prepared baking sheets, 12 strips to a sheet, spaced 1 inch apart.

5. Bake for 15 to 20 minutes, or until the edges are light brown. Let cool on the baking sheets for 20 minutes. Carefully transfer to wire racks to cool completely for about 30 minutes. These are sturdy when completely cooled but a bit fragile when warm.

WHAT YOU NEED TO KNOW: Use a box grater or shredding attachment on a food processor to shred your own cheese. Freshly shredded cheese melts better than packaged shredded cheese. The anti-caking powder used to keep it from clumping in the bag inhibits melting.

HELPFUL HINT: Although ¼ teaspoon of cayenne doesn't sound like much for 24 cheese straws, the flavor builds. It's rare anyone eats just one and the heat can sneak up on you. Try the recipe first with ⅛ teaspoon cayenne and increase the amount if you like it hotter.

SEEDED WHOLE-GRAIN ROLLS

PREP TIME: 1 hour
30 minutes
BAKE TIME: 25 minutes,
plus 30 minutes to cool

MAKES 8 SANDWICH ROLLS
NUT-FREE, WHOLE GRAIN

Of all the commercially available gluten-free bread products, one I can rarely find is a seeded sandwich roll. Not a soft, light bread roll, not a hamburger bun, but a roll meant for a filling sandwich. This recipe is for exactly that roll—one large enough to pile high with all your favorite sandwich ingredients and that won't fall apart after a generous smear of mayonnaise and mustard.

1 cup (240 ml) water,
   warmed to 95° F
2 (2.5-ounce; 7-gram)
   packets active dry yeast
3 teaspoons granulated
   sugar, divided
3 cups (405 grams)
   Gluten-Free Bread Flour
   Blend (page 13)
3 tablespoons (45 grams)
   psyllium husk powder
2 teaspoons baking powder
1 teaspoon xanthan gum
1 teaspoon baking soda
2 large eggs

1. In a small bowl, stir together the water, yeast, and 1 teaspoon of sugar. Let sit for 10 minutes to bloom the yeast (it will bubble lightly).

2. Meanwhile, in a large mixing bowl, stir together the flour blend, psyllium husk powder, remaining 2 teaspoons of sugar, baking powder, xanthan gum, and baking soda to combine.

3. To the dry ingredients, add the yeast mixture, the eggs, milk, ¼ cup (60 ml) of oil, and the vinegar. Using a handheld electric mixer on medium speed, mix for about 3 minutes, or until a sticky dough forms.

4. Line two baking sheets with parchment paper.

CONTINUED

1 cup (240 ml) whole milk or unsweetened dairy-free milk

½ cup (120 ml) grapeseed oil or vegetable oil, divided, plus more for your hands

1 teaspoon apple cider vinegar

¼ cup seeds (weight varies; such as sesame, poppy, sunflower, or a combination)

5. Coat your hands with a bit of oil and separate the dough into eight equal balls. Place four dough balls onto each baking sheet, slightly flattening to make them 4 inches in diameter, spacing them 3 inches apart. Cover with a damp kitchen towel and let rise in a warm place for about 1 hour, or until the rolls are 50 percent larger.

6. During the last 10 minutes of rising, preheat the oven to 400°F.

7. Uncover the rolls. Using a pastry brush, gently brush the tops of the rolls with the remaining ¼ cup (60 ml) of oil. Sprinkle a generous teaspoon of the seeds on top of each roll.

8. Place both sheets in the oven and bake for 22 to 25 minutes, or until the rolls are browned and feel firm when lightly tapped in the center. The internal temperature of the rolls tested with a thermometer should reach 185°F. Cool on a wire rack for 30 minutes before slicing.

WHAT YOU NEED TO KNOW: Experiment with the seeds for topping these rolls. In the cooler months, I like seeds with a little more depth of flavor, like fennel and flax. Beyond sesame, poppy, and sunflower seeds, try black sesame, pumpkin, chia, or hemp seeds.

MOM'S DINNER ROLLS

These are the dinner rolls I grew up eating at holiday meals, made from a handwritten recipe on an index card in my mom's treasured recipe box. Like many recipes, I found out later in life, it was a common recipe for butterhorn rolls many families had claimed as their own. I spent the first few holidays after being diagnosed with celiac disease experimenting to make this recipe work without gluten. Now, the result is flaky, buttery, and soft—just like the rolls I grew up eating.

PREP TIME: 30 minutes, plus 8 hours to rise
BAKE TIME: 12 minutes, plus 10 minutes to cool

MAKES 16 ROLLS

DAIRY-FREE OPTION, NUT-FREE

½ cup (120 ml) whole milk, at room temperature

¼ cup (60 ml) water, warmed to 95°F

1 (2.5-ounce; 7-gram) packet active dry yeast

4 tablespoons (55 grams) granulated sugar, divided

2¼ cups (304 grams) Gluten-Free Bread Flour Blend (page 13)

1 tablespoon psyllium husk powder

1. In a small bowl, stir together the milk, water, yeast, and 1 tablespoon of sugar. Let sit for 10 minutes to bloom the yeast (it will bubble lightly).

2. Meanwhile, in a large mixing bowl, stir together the flour blend, remaining 3 tablespoons (41.25 grams) of sugar, psyllium husk powder, salt, and xanthan gum to combine.

3. Add the cold cubed butter. Using a pastry cutter or two forks, work the butter into the dry mixture until you reach a coarse crumble with pea-size pieces of butter.

CONTINUED

1 teaspoon fine sea salt

½ teaspoon xanthan gum

3 tablespoons (42 grams)
cold unsalted
butter, cubed

1 large egg

4 tablespoons (½ stick;
60 ml) melted unsalted
butter, divided

4. To the flour mixture, add the egg and yeast mixture. Using a wooden spoon, mix well, stirring for 3 to 5 minutes, or until the mixture forms a slightly sticky dough.

5. Have 2 tablespoons (30 ml) of melted butter ready with a pastry brush.

6. Line two baking sheets with parchment paper.

7. Divide the dough into two equal portions. Place one portion on a large piece of plastic wrap. Refrigerate the second portion until needed. Place another piece of plastic wrap over the top of the dough and gently pat it into a disk, then roll it into an 8-inch circle. Remove the top piece of plastic.

8. Brush the dough circle with 1 tablespoon of melted butter. Using a knife or pizza cutter, cut the dough into eight equal wedges. Roll the wedges, starting at the wide outside edge and rolling it into the center. Place the rolls onto one of the prepared baking sheets 2 inches apart. Repeat with the second dough portion.

9. Cover the rolls with a damp kitchen towel and let rise in a warm area overnight until the rolls are 50 percent larger.

10. When ready to bake, preheat the oven to 375°F.

11. Using a pastry brush, brush the rolls with the remaining 2 tablespoons (30 ml) of melted butter.

12. Bake for 10 to 12 minutes, or until the rolls are lightly browned. Cool on a wire rack for 10 minutes before eating. These rolls may be served warm.

WHAT YOU NEED TO KNOW: This dough is a good substitute in recipes that call for canned crescent rolls. This recipe is equivalent to two cans of crescent rolls; however, they do not rise as fast as those in the can.

MAKE IT DAIRY-FREE: Use equal amounts of unsweetened dairy-free milk (such as almond milk, if nuts are not an issue) and dairy-free butter (such as Earth Balance).

GARLIC KNOTS

PREP TIME: 30 minutes, plus 30 minutes to rise
BAKE TIME: 20 minutes

MAKES 10 KNOTS

DAIRY-FREE OPTION, EGG-FREE, NUT-FREE, VEGAN OPTION

If you've had garlic knots at a New York–style pizzeria, you already know how flavorful and hard to pass up these are! I like to serve them as an appetizer while a pizza is baking, along with a side of marinara sauce or garlic butter for dipping.

2½ cups (337.5 grams) plus 2 tablespoons (17 grams) Gluten-Free Bread Flour Blend (page 13), divided

1 tablespoon psyllium husk powder

1 (2.5-ounce; 7-gram) packet instant yeast

1 teaspoon granulated sugar

½ teaspoon sea salt

1¼ cups (300 ml) water

1 tablespoon olive oil or grapeseed oil

2 tablespoons (30 ml) melted unsalted butter

1 tablespoon minced garlic

1 teaspoon dried oregano

1. Preheat the oven to 425°F. Line a baking sheet with parchment paper.

2. In a medium mixing bowl, whisk together 2½ cups (337.5 grams) of flour blend, the psyllium husk powder, yeast, sugar, and salt to combine. Stir in the water and oil until a dough forms.

3. Sprinkle the remaining 2 tablespoons (17 grams) of flour blend on a work surface. Divide the dough into 10 equal portions. Using your hands, roll each portion into an 8-inch log. Tie each log into a knot like you would a piece of string, crossing one end over the other and gently pulling it through the loop. Place the knots on the prepared baking sheet, 1 inch apart. Cover with a damp kitchen towel and let rise in a warm place for about 30 minutes, or until the knots are 50 percent larger.

4. In a small bowl, stir together the melted butter, garlic, and oregano. When the rolls are ready to go in the oven, brush them with half the butter mixture.

5. Bake for 18 to 20 minutes, or until lightly browned and their internal temperature tested with a thermometer reaches 185°F. Remove from the oven and immediately brush with the remaining butter mixture. Serve immediately.

WHAT YOU NEED TO KNOW: This recipe also makes two (8-inch) pizza crusts. Instead of rolling into knots, pat half the dough into an 8-inch circle. Let rise for about 20 minutes, or until the dough is 2 inches taller. Brush with the oil and bake at 425°F for 10 minutes. Top with sauce, cheese, and toppings and bake for about another 10 minutes, or until the cheese melts.

MAKE IT DAIRY-FREE AND VEGAN: Replace the butter with an equal amount of dairy-free butter (such as Earth Balance).

MEASUREMENT CONVERSIONS

VOLUME EQUIVALENTS	U.S. STANDARD	U.S. STANDARD (OUNCES)	METRIC (APPROXIMATE)
LIQUID	2 tablespoons	1 fl. oz.	30 mL
	¼ cup	2 fl. oz.	60 mL
	½ cup	4 fl. oz.	120 mL
	1 cup	8 fl. oz.	240 mL
	1½ cups	12 fl. oz.	355 mL
	2 cups or 1 pint	16 fl. oz.	475 mL
	4 cups or 1 quart	32 fl. oz.	1 L
	1 gallon	128 fl. oz.	4 L
DRY	⅛ teaspoon	—	0.5 mL
	¼ teaspoon	—	1 mL
	½ teaspoon	—	2 mL
	¾ teaspoon	—	4 mL
	1 teaspoon	—	5 mL
	1 tablespoon	—	15 mL
	¼ cup	—	59 mL
	⅓ cup	—	79 mL
	½ cup	—	118 mL
	⅔ cup	—	156 mL
	¾ cup	—	177 mL
	1 cup	—	235 mL
	2 cups or 1 pint	—	475 mL
	3 cups	—	700 mL
	4 cups or 1 quart	—	1 L
	½ gallon	—	2 L
	1 gallon	—	4 L

OVEN TEMPERATURES

FAHRENHEIT	CELSIUS (APPROXIMATE)
250°F	120°C
300°F	150°C
325°F	165°C
350°F	180°C
375°F	190°C
400°F	200°C
425°F	220°C
450°F	230°C

WEIGHT EQUIVALENTS

U.S. STANDARD	METRIC (APPROXIMATE)
½ ounce	15 g
1 ounce	30 g
2 ounces	60 g
4 ounces	115 g
8 ounces	225 g
12 ounces	340 g
16 ounces or 1 pound	455 g

RESOURCES

STORE-BOUGHT GLUTEN-FREE FLOUR BLENDS

In addition to the gluten-free flour blend recipes I've provided in this book (see pages 12-14), there are several store-bought gluten-free flour blends I find useful and effective.

Better Batter All-Purpose Flour Mix makes fantastic biscuits if you find yourself out of my flour blend. It has a light, fluffy mixture.

Cup4Cup Multipurpose Flour has a smooth, silky texture due to its high cornstarch content. This flour blend does contain dairy, which helps replace the protein lost when eliminating gluten in flour but may not be suitable if you're dairy intolerant.

gfJules Gluten-Free All-Purpose Flour and mixes are good choices when avoiding any of the top eight allergens in addition to gluten. Jules carefully sources all her ingredients and makes her blends in a dedicated gluten-free facility.

King Arthur Gluten-Free All-Purpose Flour is made without xanthan gum or guar gum. This is a lovely blend for muffins, waffles, and quick breads, creating a nice crumb.

Namaste Perfect Flour Blend is a terrific flour blend for those seeking a whole-grain option.

Trader Joe's Baker Josef's Gluten-Free All-Purpose Flour is my go-to if I need a quick substitution for my Johnna's Favorite Gluten-Free All-Purpose Flour Blend (page 12). It does not contain any xanthan gum or guar gum, which makes it ideal since not all recipes use the same amount of gums per cup.

GUIDE TO HIGH-ALTITUDE BAKING

With high altitude comes low air pressure, meaning baked goods may not react the same way they do at sea level. If you are new to baking at high altitudes, cookies, piecrusts, and crackers are ideal places to begin. With shorter bake times than cakes and breads, they are not as susceptible to the loss of moisture and other challenges of high-altitude baking. If you first try the recipe as written and find it needs adjustment, here is a guide to help you.

Baking powder and baking soda: will need to be reduced in recipes based on your elevation. If the recipe calls for 1 teaspoon, reduce that to ⅔ teaspoon at 3,000 to 5,000 feet, ½ teaspoon at 5,000 to 6,000 feet, and ¼ teaspoon at 6,500 to 8,000 feet.

Baking time: should be decreased by 5 to 7 minutes for each 30 minutes of baking time. For example, if a cake recipe calls for 30 minutes in the oven, decrease the baking time to 23 to 25 minutes. The lower air pressure at higher elevation makes baking happen quicker.

Flour: an additional 1 tablespoon of flour may be helpful in recipes baked above 3,500 feet. For each additional 1,500 feet in elevation, add 1 tablespoon of flour.

Liquid: increase the liquid in a recipe by 1 to 2 tablespoons (15 to 30 ml) at 3,000-feet elevation. Above 3,000 feet, increase the liquid by 1½ teaspoons for each additional 1,000 feet of elevation to address evaporation.

Oven temperature: can be increased by 15°F for most baked goods and by 25°F when making cakes or chocolate-containing treats. A higher temperature provides a quick set to your baked goods, reducing the amount of moisture lost during baking.

Sugar: reduce the amount of sugar in a recipe by 1 tablespoon per cup. The reason for this is much like oven temperature—more sugar increases the evaporation in baked goods. Lowering the amount of sugar may strengthen the structure and keep it moist.

To learn more about high-altitude baking, I recommend the Colorado State University Extension's *High Altitude Food Preparation Guide,* available for no charge online.

INDEX

ACKNOWLEDGMENTS

When I began writing this book, I was concerned it would be a very solitary project. I could not have been more wrong and am so grateful to have shared the experience with people who make my heart full.

To my favorite fella, John, you are always there when the dishes are overwhelming after a baking marathon, to taste test a new recipe, to find missing ingredients in the midst of a pandemic, and to hold the rest of our lives together when I decide to bake or write all night. I can only do this because of your support. Love you lots.

To my dear friend Shirley Braden, it is because of your website, *Gluten Free Easily*, your gentle guidance and real-world recipes, and your encouragement and ability to create connections in the gluten-free community that I am thriving with celiac disease. To be welcomed into your kitchen is something I treasure. You inspire me to do the same for others.

To each of you who offered encouragement and input in a decade-long journey of gluten-free baking, I heard you and appreciate you. Renee, Laurie, Lisa, Kristin, Sue, and Kathy, you keep me afloat. Mary, Karen, Celeste, and Dawn, your collective bread knowledge is cherished. Bill and Christina, you've been the support all gluten-free eaters need and have made shared meals possible.

Just like dessert, saving the best for last, the publishing team behind this book. This book is what I wish had been waiting at the bookstore the day I was diagnosed with celiac disease. They had the vision to make this book happen, to guide me along the way and make this possible. Grateful.

ABOUT THE AUTHOR

Johnna Wright Perry is the creator of the website *In Johnna's Kitchen*. She lives near Kansas City, Missouri, with her husband, a pack of mismatched rescue dogs, and a tiny flock of backyard chickens. When she isn't in the kitchen, she travels around the globe chasing sunsets and the best gluten-free croissants and pizza.

CPSIA information can be obtained
at www.ICGtesting.com
Printed in the USA
JSHW021552020521
14138JS00004B/4